Retention
And Its Prevention

Making Informed Decisions
About Individual Children

by

Jim Grant

PUBLISHED BY
MODERN LEARNING PRESS
ROSEMONT, NEW JERSEY

ISBN 1-56762-066-3
Copyright © 1997 by Jim Grant
Printed in the United States of America. All rights reserved. No part of this book
may be reproduced in any manner whatsoever without the written permission of the
publisher. For more information, contact Modern Learning Press, P.O. Box 167,
Rosemont, NJ 08556.
Item #438

Dedication

To my big brother, John,
who started school in September of 1946
and was assigned to a large first grade class.
As a developmentally young, left-handed male
who was forced to sit on his left hand
and write with his right hand,
he was predestined to repeat a grade.
In spite of overwhelming odds,
he went on to enjoy a very productive life.

Special Thanks

To Robert Low,
my good friend and editor,
and a world-class wordsmith,
&
To Jay LaRoche, Irv Richardson,
and my wife, Lillian,whose
extra hard work provided the additional time
I needed to work on this project.

Contents

Preface

In 1989, my first book about grade-level retention was published. Called *Worth Repeating*, it explained why and how some young children need to spend an additional year in the same grade so that they can succeed in school.

Even before *Worth Repeating* was published, efforts were being made to prohibit the use of retention and other extra-year options in schools across America. As is explained further in this book, these efforts soon took the form of a negative media campaign very similar to the types of campaigns increasingly being used by politicians at about the same time. In the years that followed, additional learning time for children stopped simply being an educational strategy and instead became a political and economic issue, as well.

In the meantime, the condition of many American children was also changing in new and often surprising ways, which increased the need for schools to have options that provided additional time to learn and grow. But, because many schools did not provide such options or parents chose not to take advantage of them, many children were socially promoted from grade to grade without having learned needed information and skills.

The extent of the changes that occurred in regard to retention led me to conclude that rather than just revising *Worth Repeating*, I needed to create a new book that would draw on the previous material but also include a great deal of new information presented in new ways, in order to help parents and educators gain a truly contemporary perspective on what has become an extremely important and controversial issue. For rather than being outlawed and abandoned, retention continues to be a widely used educational strategy—and one that is receiving even greater attention as large numbers of parents, educators, politicians, and business executives all call for the use of high standards to make sure that students learn what they need to know before proceeding to the next grade level.

If anyone still had doubts about both the educational and political importance of retention, those doubts were probably put to rest on February 4th, 1997, when the President of the United States included the following paragraph in the official text of his State of the Union Message:

> *"Raising standards will not be easy, and some of our children will not be able to meet them at first. The point is not to put our children down, but to lift them up. Good tests will show us who needs help, what changes in teaching to make and which schools to improve. They can help us to end social promotion. For no child should move from grade school to junior high, or junior high to high school, until he or she is ready."*

Now, let's consider why some children may need additional learning time in order to become ready, and what we can do to help these children achieve success in school.

Introduction

"We must promote every one of our students every year, whether or not they have done the required work or are ready to succeed in the next grade."

"Our students' self-esteem depends solely on their being promoted at the end of the year, not on their ability to understand or do their work every day."

"If we provide any of our students with an additional year to learn under any circumstances, they are almost certain to drop out of school, because keeping children with their classmates is far more important than enabling them to learn needed information and skills."

Do you believe this stuff?

I sure don't. And, the overwhelming majority of the thousands of teachers, administrators, and parents I talk with every year don't believe it, either.

Why? It just doesn't make sense, and it doesn't reflect the realities adults and children experience in schools across America every day.

Of course, it should come as no surprise that there is a group of extremists who believe—or, at least, support—the positions described above. These days, you can always find a group of ideological purists who claim there is only one right way for everyone, and no exceptions or compromises with differing points of view should be allowed.

But, what is surprising—and perhaps even downright horrifying— is that the positions described above have in fact become *policy* at public schools in various parts of the country, even though these outlandish ideas don't have public support and just don't make sense.

How did this happen?

Throughout most of the 1970s and 1980s, a very small number of students might have spent a second year in the same grade, while some other students participated in extra-year classes which provided a "half-step" between two grades. Many educators and parents found that this additional learning time helped many (though not all) students succeed in school, which is why these practices became so widespread and commonplace. Then, in the late 1980s a negative media campaign launched by a small but influential group of education bureaucrats and university professors succeeded in spreading the idea that taking an extra year to learn did *not* help struggling young students and instead was likely to turn them into high school drop-outs.

Amazingly enough, the national news media—including many education publications—fell for the flawed data and pious press releases issued by the supposed protectors of America's youth. And, as a result, a great many extra-year classes were abolished, even though numerous studies showed they provided significant educational benefits to many participants. In addition, many teachers were told that they should not and could not retain *any* students.

Hard to believe?

Consider the following transcript of a phone call made to me when I appeared on a television talk show. And, consider the impact on a nationwide audience when a distraught mother named Sharon told us all:

"My son was a young five when he entered kindergarten. Mentally he was fine, but physically he kept getting tired, and he cried the whole year. He was not physically ready. I felt and my husband felt that we should have kept him back, but his teacher said, 'Just push him along, and in first grade if there's a problem, we'll make an adjustment.' But nothing was done. Now he's in second grade, he's still not physically ready, and he's the smallest in his class. He feels physically not ready for what second grade has for him."

—from the "Parents Helper" show on America's Talking Television, September 25, 1995.

Not convinced? Nothing to worry about? Just an isolated incident?

Well, consider what I was told not so long ago by a second grade teacher. She and a child's parents all wanted the child to repeat second grade, but her principal told her that under no circumstances would she be allowed to retain the child. "The principal refutes everything I say by telling me what the research says," she told me. And, this caring teacher has also been told that if she simply meets the individual needs of her students, they won't have any need for extra time.

Just a coincidence?

Get real. Here's what's actually happening:

"Social promotion, as this practice is known, is less popular than it used to be. It is even against the law in some places. Nevertheless, polls of teachers show that social promotion is alive and well in schools across the country. For example, according to a recent survey of Texas teachers,

- *68 percent of elementary school teachers had students who were promoted to the next grade level even though they failed the class.*

- *61 percent of middle school and junior high teachers had students who failed the course and were allowed to move on without repeating it.*

- *40 percent said that a student they had recommended for retention was promoted.*

- *78 percent disagreed with a statement that students in their school are not promoted unless they have earned the necessary passing grades.*

These figures are stark but other surveys, both national and state, tell a similar story of promoting students who are unprepared."

—from a March, 1996 paid advertisement entitled "Passing on Failure" by Albert Shanker, President of the American Federation of Teachers.

If you talk with large numbers of teachers and parents across America, like I do every year, you know that situations like these occur in all too many public schools. And, what is especially different and shameful about many of these situations is that they are not just social promotion, which has now been condemned by a President of the United States, as well as a President of the American Federation of Teachers. They are examples of *forced social promotion* being carried out in a secretive and insidious way.

Traditional social promotion, which was bad enough, usually resulted from a parent's and/or child's desire for continued progress through the grades. Now, however, even when the parents, teacher, and child all agree that an extra year in the same grade will help the child learn needed material and feel better about being in school, an administrator who has no firsthand knowledge of the situation may *force* the child to continue moving on from grade to grade—no matter how unhappy the child is, no matter how far behind the child has fallen, and regardless of whether the child can reasonably be expected to learn successfully in each grade.

Why would an administrator responsible for the education of our children do such a thing?

How about a quick, one-word answer: **MONEY**. As the relentless pressure to tighten budgets has forced administrators to scrutinize every penny, more than one bean-counting bureaucrat has figured out that giving a child an extra year in school represents a cost of about $5,000 or so. And, having succeeded in learning the multiplication tables at some point in his or her career, this sort of financial wizard has also determined that if 200 children in a large district are retained each year, the total annual cost comes to about *one million dollars.*

Armed with these figures, some misleading information about additional learning time, and the dubious wisdom that schools are now supposed to act more like businesses, this sort of bottom-line bureaucrat can use the same quick and dirty way to cut costs favored by certain corporations: *downsizing*. Of course, school administrators can't just fire large numbers of students, but forcing every student to go from kindergarten through 12th grade in only 13 years is one way to downsize the overall student population.

However, there are a few problems with this economic model. One problem is that forcing students to move on to a new grade before they are ready often leads to increased spending on remediation, special education, and other programs, which are likely to be just as expensive but less effective than another year in a regular classroom.

Another problem is that those same parents whose understanding of and concern for their child is so inappropriately ignored are also likely to be taxpayers—the same folks who are frequently asked to provide school districts with increased funding. (In business terms, they might be considered both customers and stockholders.) Are the parents described above likely to support the administrator's next funding recommendations? And, are other taxpayers likely to approve school budgets, when their neighbors and the media keep telling them that significant numbers of students are being promoted each year without having learned basic skills? I don't think so.

Most of all, this sort of policy just happens to be morally wrong, because it hurts kids and ignores the firsthand knowledge of those who are closest to the children and responsible for their education: parents and classroom teachers. In the words of Albert Shanker, the President of the American Federation of Teachers cited earlier, social promotion "cheats" children. And, all the talk about values and character education rings very hollow when the people responsible for running a public school are deliberately depriving a significant number of students of needed time to learn.

In addition, it is no accident that the widespread calls for high standards have been coupled with condemnations of social promotion. A school-wide social promotion policy results in the school's only standards being continued attendance and breathing. Any sort of standard based on learning requires a willingness to provide extra time for children who have not yet succeeded in meeting the standards.

So, what do we do about children who don't meet standards, or who are obviously and unhappily in the wrong grade even though they're scraping by academically?

That's what this book is all about. And, in a nutshell, what this book explains is that rather than relying on forced social promotion, schools can and do offer students who need additional learning time a variety of helpful options, including remaining in the same classroom with the same teacher for another year. The key to the success of these extra-time programs is making informed decisions about the specific needs of individual children—and then determining which programs best meet those needs.

This is not always easy, but as educators and parents, we have a responsibility to do our best for struggling young students, rather than refusing to let them have the learning time they need, and then promoting them from one grade to another in which they cannot succeed.

Chapter I

Welcome To Your School System!
Would *You* Want To Spend An Extra Year In It?

"All school entrance and grade placement decisions will be based solely on the number of candles on each child's birthday cake. Each child will then have no more than 180 days to learn the material required for promotion to the next grade level. And, all children will proceed through the grades at the exact same rate, regardless of their individual needs or differences. Any child who takes more than 13 years to go from kindergarten through 12th grade is a failure."

Does this sound like the American way?

Well, as a matter of fact, it's really the Prussian way, which Horace Mann brought to the United States way back in the 1840s. Its origin may help to explain why it is frequently described as a "lock-step" approach to education, with each participant expected to march forward at exactly the same pace as every other participant.

This approach has also been compared to a "factory" or "assembly line," and it's probably no coincidence that this school system was developed during the Industrial Revolution and designed to help prepare young people for factory jobs. It's also no coincidence that this approach was developed in a European autocracy that tended to regiment its citizens rather than "celebrate their differences."

But, even so, it's our system now, and it's done a great job of educating Americans for over one hundred and fifty years, right?

Well, not exactly. Consider some information about the success rate of our elementary schools during the first half of the twentieth century:

> "...in 1909 the average rate for nonpromotion in all elementary grades was 16 percent (Ayres 1909). A study by Caswell (1933) about 55 years ago revealed that the average rate of nonpromotion in elementary schools had dropped to 10 percent. Obviously, these statistics are somewhat misleading since mandatory attendance laws are a relatively recent innovation, and in past years problem students may have dropped out of school instead of being retained."

—Light's Retention Scale Manual by Wayne Light, Ph.D.

Oops! As many as one out of every seven students were failing and repeating a grade back in the "good old days." And, way back then you could even find some major "chronological anomalies," such as a 12-year-old who was still in third grade, perhaps because he just couldn't get those multiplication tables figured out.

Of course, we know much more than we did back then, so someone must have fixed the system and reduced the retention rate by now, right?

Well, here's an example of the sort of data that has been published in professional journals and distributed to educators nationwide in recent years:

> "Grade failure rates are as high as they were in the 19th century, before the days of social promotion: Although annual statistics show only about a 6 percent annual percentage rate for retention, year after year that produces a cumulative rate of nonpromotion greater

than 50 percent. By ninth grade approximately half of all students in the U.S. have flunked at least one grade (or are no longer in school)."

—"Synthesis of Research on Grade Retention" by Lorrie Shepard & Mary Lee Smith, *Educational Leadership*, May, 1990.

Now, it could be that half the students in your local school have flunked at least one grade, but that's certainly not the case at my local school. And, none of the tens of thousands of educators I've talked with during the last three decades have ever told me about anything close to a 50 percent retention rate in their school systems, either. Of course, in this sort of situation I tend to believe people who actually work with students more than I believe university professors who "synthesize" research, especially when the professors' data seems to defy common sense. (And, if you're thinking that a few big city school systems might be skewing the numbers, on page 88 of this book you'll find a quote from *The Los Angeles Times* stating that the retention rate for middle schools in the Los Angeles Unified School District is under *one* percent.)

But, whatever the accuracy of the statistics cited above, I think it's safe to say that retention is not just some little flaw in the system that we can easily eliminate. Even if the annual nationwide retention rate is only one percent—a far more believable figure—now that we have close to 50 million American children going to school, approximately half a million students are being retained each year.

How could so many children still be "failed" by their school system after all this time?

Well, much like the original assembly lines, the original Prussian/American, lock-step school system is very intolerant of any individual's need for extra time. If a particular child needs two or three months more to master the same material as the other children in the class, that child must either be promoted at the end of the school year without having learned everything needed to succeed in the next grade, or that child must be given a whole extra year in the same grade that didn't work so well the first time around. It's a rigid, "either/or" approach with no middle ground, even though the middle ground is exactly where many children land, and where the most effective solutions can often be found.

Now, you may be thinking that if the rigid, lock-step school system is the root of the problem, why not just change the system? My answer is that you may succeed where so many others have failed, but so far this old school system of ours has remained essentially intact despite innumerable attempts to change it. And, while that doesn't mean any of us should stop trying, it does mean that we have a responsibility to make the best possible decisions for the individual children who are now in the system and need our help *today*.

In my experience, too many idealistic reformers have been willing to sacrifice children they don't personally know in order to achieve a "better tomorrow"—which somehow never quite seems to arrive. In particular, some ideological extremists like to argue that perpetuating retention and other extra-time options helps to keep the system going, so we have to get rid of the alternatives in order to change the system. However, I believe in using the system to help children change and grow, not using children to help the system change and grow. That's why I firmly believe that retention and other extra-time options must remain available until we've not only reformed the school system completely, but also confirmed that our reforms work perfectly for every single child.

As that day does not seem to be coming any time soon, we now need to gain a more detailed understanding of what's really going on within this wonderful system of ours, so that we can make informed and appropriate decisions for the children in our care. And, I hope you won't be totally shocked and dismayed if I suggest that the process of evaluating and meeting children's educational needs is not quite as pure and simple as we all would like it to be.

"Our timebound mentality has forced us into believing that schools can educate all of the people all of the time in a school year of 180 six-hour days. The consequence of our self-deception has been to ask the impossible of our students."

—Report of the National Education Commission on Time and Learning, 1994.

The Politics & Economics Of Your School System

You've probably figured out already that the amount of time a particular child needs to learn something does not depend solely on the child. Much depends on what and how the child is taught. And, while these considerations have long been contentious educational issues, in recent years they have also become contentious political issues. At the same time, the economics of funding our school system has also become politicized, and financial factors have been shown to have a powerful impact on the rate at which students learn. So, in trying to sort out what's really happening in our schools, we now have to keep a watchful eye out for unfortunate by-products of the political process, including misleading propaganda, negative media campaigns, and deliberate disinformation, such as the following:

"Classroom teachers decide what is taught in their classrooms and can 'individualize' what and how they teach, in order to meet the needs of each student and prevent any student from ever needing an extra year of school."

If you believe the preceding statement, I feel I have a responsibility to warn you that neither the Tooth Fairy, Santa Claus, nor any classroom teacher really has the sole responsibility for deciding what and how they deliver to children. Furthermore, I would warn you to be extremely suspicious of anyone who actually claims to be the Tooth Fairy, Santa Claus, or an educator who can prevent all children from ever needing an extra year to grow and learn in school.

, for better or worse, is that upper-level school district
ther education administrators make many of the deci-
...s regarding the curriculum and how it should be taught in a particular classroom. In addition, the publishers of the books and
standardized tests used throughout a grade or school also wield tremendous influence within any classroom where the teacher must
make sure that children learn large amounts of what is in the books and
on the tests.

Last but certainly not least, many politicians and special interest
groups have also taken it upon themselves to decide what and how
young children should be taught. In their infinite wisdom and through
myriad mandates, these "education experts" have decided that many
classroom teachers not only can but *must* teach their elementary-grade
students about proper nutrition, drug and alcohol abuse, good and bad
touches, saving the environment, gun safety, and a number of other
topics that many grown-ups have obviously not yet mastered.

Now, before you put me down as some sort of "back-to-basics"
Neanderthal, please understand the point I am trying to make, which
is that when I started out as a teacher at an elementary school, my fellow teachers and I were required to teach *none* of the topics just listed.
And, of course, that did leave us more time to teach our students sub-
jects such as reading, writing, and 'rithmetic.

The end result of all the meddling and mandates since then is what
I call the "upholstery curriculum," because it's very well padded and
covers everything. However, my colleague, Bob Johnson, who has also
been an elementary school teacher and principal, sees things differently. He thinks it should be called the "constipation curriculum,"
because people keep stuffing more in and never eliminate anything.

Whatever it should be called, the curriculum has expanded greatly
in recent times, while the 180-day periods in which it must be taught
each year have not. So, common sense would seem to suggest that

some children are going to need more time to learn so much additional material, or will just learn some things less well.

At the same time that the elementary curriculum has been expanding, the level of its subject matter has been going up and down like a championship yo-yo. In fact, this upward and downward mobility has actually been going on even longer than the curriculum expansion, and these curriculum-level changes have often been directly linked to changes in policies regarding extra time to learn.

Back in the early 1950s, kindergarten in particular tended to be a gentle and relaxed place, where the emphasis was on fostering social development and the transition from home to school. Then, after the Russians won the first round of the space race by sending Sputnik into orbit in 1957, American "experts" decided that nationwide "education reforms" were needed to help the U.S. catch up with its foreign competition. (Sound familiar?)

Unfortunately, these "experts" used a top-down approach, starting with what college students should know and then working back down the grades from there. The result was a dramatically escalated "pushed-down" curriculum in the primary grades. This, of course, did not match the abilities of many children and put more than a few of them on the path to flunking and then dropping out of school.

By the early 1960s, a growing number of educators and parents were concerned about this trend and beginning to explore ways to help struggling children. These concerns received important new support in 1964, when *Reader's Digest* published an article by Dr. Louise Bates Ames entitled, "Is Your Child in the Wrong Grade?" This landmark article introduced a new generation to the concept of *wrong grade placement*—the idea that placing all children in a particular grade based *solely* on the child's year of birth, without considering important developmental factors, results in a significant number of children "adjusting badly to school" because they are not yet ready to succeed in a particular grade.

7

With the active support of Dr. Ames and her colleagues, schools across America began implementing a more developmental approach to education, based on matching the level and type of instruction to children's current stage of development. As part of this approach, children who were not yet ready to succeed in a particular grade could take an extra year to learn and grow early in their school career, if necessary. This extra year was often provided as a "readiness" class before kindergarten, an extra year in kindergarten, or a "transition" class between kindergarten and first grade, all of which gave chronologically or developmentally young children an additional year of learning time before the cycle of frustration, fear, and failure created a self-fulfilling pattern of negative attitudes and poor performance, which too often culminated in children flunking, being retained, and then dropping out of school years later.

This sort of developmental approach remained widespread and popular during the 1970s. In the early 1980s, however, a government report entitled *Nation At Risk* claimed that America's school system was not doing a good enough job of preparing students. Right at the same time, foreign competition was widely blamed for hurting American companies and putting many Americans out of work. So, many schools introduced a new round of "education reforms," which emphasized more intensive instruction and higher-level materials, in order to help the U.S. catch up with its foreign competition. (Sound familiar?)

In the late 1980s, the predictable reaction occurred, with a new group of reformers promoting "developmentally appropriate practices" that included a de-escalated curriculum. The new wrinkle this time, however, was that the negative media campaign used to gain attention for their program attacked the extra-year options which were essential elements of the traditional developmental approach. A few university professors and education bureaucrats quoted repeatedly as part of this campaign also promoted the ideas that any extra-year programs for children should be considered "retention," and that the effects of being developmentally or chronologically young would disappear by third grade.

"A recent review of all the research suggests that the effects of being the youngest disappear by the end of third grade (Shepard & Smith, 1986)."

—*Young Children Magazine*, May, 1990.

"There are no comprehensive figures on how common extra-year programs are, but Dr. Shepard estimated that at their height in the late 1980s, as many as one-third of all school districts had them. She said her sense was that the number had decreased since then, in part because the National Association for the Education of Young Children spread information that the extra-year classes were inappropriate."

—*The New York Times*, December 28, 1994.

This round of "reforms" led to a more play-oriented approach to learning being used in many schools, combined with an increased emphasis on self-esteem, a decreased emphasis on learning skills, and a prohibition on providing any extra-time options, including retention. The thoroughly predictable result was that many students who were just "taken where they are and moved along from there" ended up being woefully unprepared to succeed in the lock-step, high-pressure grade structure of the intermediate and upper grades, making these children prime candidates to flunk and be retained at a later and more damaging stage of their school careers. And, as might be expected, educators and parents across America have since found that too many children did *not* suddenly and magically catch up with everyone else in third grade.

"If you still think all these struggling kids are going to catch up in third grade, fourth grade, or any other grade, you have some catching up of your own to do."

—Bob Johnson, education consultant.

By the mid-1990s, a wide variety of organizations were claiming that a new round of "education reforms," which included higher-level materials and strict standards, were needed to help the U.S. keep up with its foreign competitors in the "new global economy." (Sound familiar?) Unfortunately, at the same time a growing number of teachers were finding that grade-level materials they formerly used were now beyond the capabilities of many students, who still needed more time to grow and learn before they could use them successfully.

Of course, common sense would seem to suggest that if schools insist on higher-level materials and strict standards under these circumstances, some "curriculum-disabled" children are going to need more time to grow and learn in school.

As if the overall expansion and constant up-and-down movement of the curriculum weren't enough, there have also been wide pendulum swings in the types of methods used to teach children in the elementary grades. (If all these different types of changes are starting to make you feel a little dizzy, you're getting a sense of what it's like to be an elementary school teacher in America. Now, imagine all this is happening at the same time that 25 or 30 high-energy kids are spending their days in the same room with you, and you may start to understand why so many teachers are taking early retirement or moving on to other professions.)

The teaching of reading and writing probably offers the most infamous example of the "swinging pendulum" effect. Especially in California during the 1980s, the traditional phonics-oriented approach was largely and officially abandoned, and a "whole language" approach implemented instead. This made sense in some respects, because the use of boring basal readers ("See the dog. See the dog run.") and equally uninspired instruction techniques (often called the "drill, skill, and kill" approach) did not foster interest, enthusiasm, or competence among many emerging readers and writers. But, in other respects, the decision to opt for wholesale abandonment rather than ongoing improvement turned out to be a grave error, because an understanding of phonics appears to be vital for many students.

In addition, while the whole language approach appeared to work well in some other countries and in some "controlled studies," it had not been thoroughly tested in a wide variety of American schools, or integrated with the curriculum in the intermediate and upper grades. As a result, some students learned to read and write very well with just a whole language approach, some did well initially but ran into problems when they could not "decode" more complex words in the upper grades, and some became good chanters but never really learned to read or write very well at all.

In 1995, after standardized tests showed that California's student reading scores dropped to the level where they were the second worst in the nation, the state announced that it was implementing a new approach in which both phonics and whole language would be integrated and used. This approach included the teaching of phonics, spelling, and skills within the context of literature-based instruction, which was precisely the common-sense approach that many teachers in other parts of the country had been using all along, because it met the needs of the full range of students in their classes, and because it supported both the interest and skills students need to become enthusiastic readers.

As with so many other issues, the real problem with the implementation of the whole language approach in California (and some other places) was the insistence of zealous extremists that they had the one and only answer for every single student in our diverse society—and that no compromise or integration with other approaches could be tolerated. As usual, the people promoting this sort of rigid, ideological stance were not really focused on meeting the differing needs of the full range of individual children in our schools.

And, the same sort of extremist, either/or approach has now been adapted by schools which refuse to provide any extra-time options, including retention, for any student. Rather than trying to improve a technique that a wide range of educators have used with varying degrees of success throughout the century, the usual sorts of "experts" claim that the approach must be totally and irrevocably abandoned for *every* student everywhere, because "the research proves" it doesn't work.

Unfortunately, however, after many years of negative campaigning against retention and other extra-time options, these "experts" are still not providing research which truly proves that the alternatives they promote, including social promotion, work well for the full range of students in a wide range of schools across America. Nor is the research on retention anywhere near as convincing and uniform as they would like you to believe.

Meanwhile, as growing numbers of intermediate and upper-grade teachers continue to find that the alleged alternatives are *not* in fact providing effective solutions, many of the administrators who once allowed retention and then disallowed it are now allowing it again.

Common sense, combined with years of practical experience, clearly suggests that retention can be disastrous for some students and a life-saver for others. A common-sense, centrist approach therefore requires educators to carefully consider the individual needs of a specific student, and then have a variety of options available, so that the people directly involved in the situation can choose the option that best meets the needs of the particular student. Of course, that is exactly the approach this book will present in later chapters.

First, however, no examination of the American school system and retention would be complete without at least some consideration of their economic aspects. And, unfortunately, some people have taken the same sort of extremist, either/or positions in regard to these difficult issues. On one side, there are groups that claim our school system is so inefficient we could spend much less money and still get better results.

On the opposing side, other groups claim that for America's children, no amount of spending is too much.

As usual, these sorts of positions contain a grain of truth which when taken to an extreme becomes so distorted that it stops making sense. For while it is true that simply spending more money will not necessarily solve all our education problems, there are also many well-documented situations where a lack of funding is causing real and even severe problems. And, while most of us truly want to do what's best for America's children, our personal budgets also tend to be stretched tight these days, so there's not a lot more we can or will pay in taxes.

In this sort of situation, it is part of our responsibility as citizens in a complex society to make difficult but fair decisions. And, that usually means we need to take a common-sense, centrist approach in regard to a specific issue, after we have sorted through the available information.

Take, for example, the question of class size, which is a key economic component of school funding because it determines how many teachers and classrooms a district needs. Common sense would seem to suggest that smaller class sizes are better, though more expensive, because they allow the teacher to devote more time and attention to each student's needs.

Ah, but consider the "research" done by some of the "education experts:"

"Eugene Glass and Mary Lee Smith found that as long as classes stay within the range of 20-40 students, reducing class size makes little difference in achievement."

—*The Harvard Education Letter,* November/December, 1990.

Now, if one of these experts' names sounds familiar, it's because she's the exact same person who says on page 3 that half of all the students in America have been retained by ninth grade, and who is also cited on page 9 as the source of the research indicating that the effects of being the youngest kid in the class disappear by the end of third grade. Of course, you'd believe any expert who claims that being the youngest or the oldest—or being in a small class or one twice as large—doesn't really matter, right?

Just asking.

Honestly, I know you're smarter than that, but what should we do about all those other people who think that whenever one or two university professors say the research shows something, it absolutely, positively has to be true?

One possibility is to show those people how different researchers often come to the exact opposite conclusions about the same question. Then, those other people might realize that common sense and a healthy skepticism have to be applied whenever research is cited as proving anything. For example, consider the results of studies on class size done in Tennessee:

> "Well-controlled, longitudinal research on Project STAR and the Lasting Benefits Study indicates that smaller classes can provide substantial gains in student achievement, especially in the early grades. The results can include higher self-esteem among students and higher morale among teachers—plus lower retention rates and less need for special education facilities."

> —"Smaller Classes Really Are Better," The American School Board Journal, May, 1992.

Make sense? Or, do you still believe that a teacher who works with students exactly 6 hours a day for 180 days can teach 40 students just as well as 20?

If not, you're probably willing to accept the possibility that 100% of the university professors are not 100% correct 100% of the time (which does seem likely, knowing that they disagree so frequently and bitterly with each other). And, you're probably also willing to acknowledge that we ought to use our own common sense and best judgment when sorting through the conflicting claims of people who work in ivory towers rather than elementary schools.

These same principles apply when we turn our attention to the economic aspects of retention.

Now, wait a minute, you may be thinking. Responsible educators making major decisions about the education of young children wouldn't let budgetary pressures influence their decisions, would they?

Well, these days it may be hard for them *not* to see retention as an economic issue. For example, a 1991 California Department of Education (CDE) report entitled *Beyond Retention* states:

> *"The costs for the state translate to more than $84 million annually for kindergarten retention alone."*

And, the first recommendation at the end of the report is:

> *"CDE and the legislature should explore ways of providing financial incentives to districts to reduce retention rates. Given the high cost to the state for retention, this would result in a net savings."*

Is retention an economic issue as well as an educational issue? You bet it is. And, while some administrators are quick to cite the "research" on the damage done by retention, they'll probably be more reluctant to tell you that their own budgetary pressures, combined with pressure from their state department of education, make the continued promotion of a failing child much more attractive *to them* than giving that child an additional year to master appropriate grade-level material.

Or, to look at another "side of the coin," the government, business, and education "leaders" determined to impose strict standards had better be ready to provide a lot of extra money to pay for the extra years of schooling that so many of today's students are going to need in order to meet strict standards.

Some people may be willing to pay the extra money, because they realize that the economics of retention transcend a narrow focus on school funding. Depending on which statistics you use, for example, the cost of an extra year of school is only about one-fifth to one-tenth as much as the cost of an extra year in prison, which is where so many of our functionally illiterate former students happen to end up. Then, too, somebody also has to pay for all those remedial courses provided by colleges and businesses—and one way or another, that somebody usually ends up being you and me.

Retention is also an economic issue because so many of the factors that lead a student to become a candidate for retention are money-related. As will be explained further in the next chapter, such factors as poor pre-natal and post-natal care, improper nutrition, and frequent changes of address can prevent a child from achieving success in school. In addition, the need of older students to work part-time jobs can be a factor.

Rather than acknowledge the importance of these and other factors, however, some opponents of retention cite the higher retention rates for minority students as proof that the practice is discriminatory. But, the logic of this claim is questionable at best. For while it is true that minorities tend to be retained more frequently than white students, it is also true that minorities tend to be found more frequently in the under-funded schools which have inadequate facilities and supplies, as well as large class sizes. And, too many minority children do not have adequate access to high-quality medical care and nutrition.

Knowing that widespread retention also costs a lot money, it would take a very "logically challenged" racist to withhold funding for education facilities, textbooks, teachers, medical care, and food, but then "discriminate" against the students by spending many millions of dollars more to keep them in school an extra year.

In fact, common sense would seem to suggest that unless some educators truly believe an extra year of school will help some minority students obtain a better education, retention should be reserved only for rich kids whose parents either pay lots of taxes or spend extra money to send their kids to expensive "prep" schools—many of which routinely provide new students with an extra year to "adjust" to their advanced curriculum.

As additional learning time may actually be needed to improve the fit between a school system and its rich or poor students, we now need to consider the disadvantages faced by the full range of students who become candidates for retention. At this point, some readers may not want to turn their attention to the actual students when we're having so much fun with the school system, but it's been my experience that people who pay attention to children can and do respond to their individual needs, while the people who don't pay attention to children tend to cite statistics, which they then use to "prove" that their approach is the one and only way for every child.

Chapter 2

Who Are These Kids?

Ready for some ancient history?

When I started teaching school in the late 1960s, only one child in the entire school building came from a "broken home." When I stopped working in the same school district about two decades later, close to 50% of all the students were no longer living with both biological parents.

An unstable family structure is just one of the factors that can result in a child needing more time to learn and master the curriculum. In addition to causing stress and distraction that can interfere with learning, a change in family structure may also lead to a loss of income, inadequate health care, and a change of address, all of which can have a very direct and negative impact on a child's performance in school, and thereby also have an impact on the educational experience of the child's classmates, as well.

> *"There's a whole new category of kid out there who emanates from a dysfunctional family...They might be involved in a family, but the family is so dysfunctional that they go to school and unload in the classroom. These problems are nonacademic and totally outside the curriculum. But the poor teacher is sitting there faced with this dilemma."*
>
> —Psychologist John C. Brady, quoted in *The Philadelphia Inquirer*, June 11, 1996.

Unfortunately, in the last few decades there has also been an increase in the prevalence of numerous other factors that can have a negative effect on a child's school performance. As a result, today's educators must now cope with a much greater number of children who have learning problems that may make them candidates for retention. Moreover, because so many children are now experiencing a number of different problems at the same time, today's educators must also cope with an increased number of children who have more serious, unique, and complex problems, due to "multiple co-occurring factors and circumstances" that undermine their overall well-being and ability to learn.

In other words, not only might a young child be struggling to overcome the effects of a family break-up, untreated ear infections, improper nutrition, and a recent move to a new home, that same child might also be struggling to overcome additional physical, social, emotional, or intellectual impediments at the same time. Meanwhile, the child must try to learn the same grade-level material in the same amount of time as another student who suffers from none of these problems, and who therefore can devote his or her full attention and capabilities to learning well in school.

Of course, you may still believe that what happens outside school property should have no impact on what happens in the classroom, or that a "good" teacher can always individualize the curriculum in order to teach every child the same material at the exact same rate. But, believe it or not, the harsh reality students and teachers across America now face is that a wide variety of problems are having a tremendous impact in the classroom—making teaching and learning far different than they were just a few decades ago. And, even the most innovative and effective teachers cannot help all of today's students overcome all of their problems and succeed in learning all of the required material in exactly 180 school days.

"I taught the children of yesteryear, and believe me, they were a lot easier to teach than today's children...Were yesteryear's children perfect? Of course not. Like today's children, they argued and whined, displayed stubbornness and occasional meanness. Sometimes, they refused to share and balked at taking turns. But, overall, their demeanor in the classroom and their attitude toward learning was nothing like that found in so many of today's classrooms."

—*Reaching & Teaching The Kids Today* by Carol Hoffman, Ed.D.

Why are teaching and learning so much more difficult in today's classrooms? Consider some of the other changes in the "condition of the kids" which I and so many other educators have witnessed in recent years.

Thirty years ago, most of the children who started school in our district stayed in the district until they left high school. In recent years, many students have moved in and out of several districts before leaving high school. Common sense would seem to suggest that a child who needs additional time to adjust to new teachers, new classmates, and a new curriculum may need additional time to master the curriculum.

"Students who had moved four or more times were, by sixth grade, a full year behind."

—"Kids, Schools Suffer from Revolving Door," *American Educator*, Spring, 1996.

Thirty years ago, most of the parents in our district stayed in the district because they had secure jobs there. In recent years, a growing lack of job security has led not just to more frequent moves, but also to more poverty and inadequate health care, as well as the sort of parental stress that sometimes leads to divorce, violence, and child abuse. Common sense would seem to suggest that young children who go through these types of experiences may need additional time to learn, because they do not have the emotional and physical well-being needed to concentrate and succeed in school.

Thirty years ago, the wages and benefits received by parents who did have jobs were usually enough to provide adequate care for the children in the family. In recent years, more children of working parents are living in poverty, and because children in these families are often ineligible for Medicaid, they are less likely to have coverage for medical care. Common sense would seem to suggest that some children who are suffering from inadequate nutrition and medical care may need more time to succeed in school, because health problems and simple discomfort may interfere with their ability to learn.

> "The population of children living in working-poor families has jumped from 3.4 million to 5.6 million in the past 20 years, according to the 1995 'Kids Count Data Book,'... [which] defines working-poor families as those in which one or both parents were employed at least 50 weeks a year and yet earned less than the 1994 federal poverty level, which was $11,821 for a family of three."

—*Education Week*, June 12, 1996.

Thirty years ago, the secure jobs held by fathers in intact families allowed most of the mothers to stay home with their children. In recent years, the need for mothers of young children to work has led to a much greater reliance on day care, which in many cases has exposed the children to a high turnover among caregivers, more illness due to contagious diseases, and less focused interest in a child's early learning experiences. Common sense would seem to suggest that some children who do not have enough of the educational and emotional experiences they need before they start school will need more of those sorts of experiences after they start school.

Thirty years ago, there were some children of French-Canadian descent in my area who needed help learning English. In recent years, the district has needed its own English-as-a-Second-Language specialist to help with children from as far away as Vietnam and Laos. Common sense would seem to suggest that a child who needs additional help in school to learn English may also need additional time to learn subjects being taught in English.

"At the beginning of 1991, Rogers [Arkansas] had 35 Limited-English-Proficient students out of 7,190 K-12 students. By 1994, it had 300 LEP students out of 8,060 students. Last year, the number of LEP children had jumped to 940 out of 9,400."

—*Education Week*, September 11, 1996.

Thirty years ago, the only visual media competing with books for children's attention were television shows like "Dennis The Menace" or "Leave It To Beaver." Now, many elementary school students have their own extensive video collections, as well as numerous electronic games and access to a multitude of cable stations, not to mention the Internet. Common sense would seem to suggest that this plethora of enticing distractions would diminish some children's interest in and time spent learning to read, and that additional time might therefore be needed to foster an interest in books and an ability to read them.

Thirty years ago, many babies born prematurely with very low birthweights did not survive. In recent years, medical advances have enabled many of these babies to survive and thrive, for which we are all thankful. Now that a significant number of these miraculous children have entered our schools, new studies are showing that many of them have problems that impede their ability to learn. Common sense would seem to suggest that some children who have these sorts of problems may need additional time to learn in school.

"Early studies on school-age kids who were small preemies find at least half have learning or attention problems...and the smaller the weight, the more likely they are to have these problems."

—A study by Dr. Forrest Bennett, published in *Pediatrics* and cited in *USA Today*.

Thirty years ago, there were about one or two children in each class who had what would now be considered "special needs." In recent years, the number of special-needs kids in each class is more likely to be in the 15 to 20% range, and even higher in some schools. Common sense would seem to suggest that some children who have special educational needs may need additional time in school in order to learn the same material as students who do not have such needs.

Thirty years ago, we did not know of any children who had been exposed to illegal drugs in the womb or during their preschool years, although there certainly may have been a few. In recent years, numerous children entering schools across America have had documented prenatal exposure to drugs such as crack cocaine, a type of drug that did not even exist 30 years ago. And, many of today's students have also been exposed to other environmental hazards—ranging from household chemicals to food additives—that also did not exist 30 years ago. Common sense would seem to suggest that some children who have suffered physical and emotional damage from these sort of experiences might need additional time to overcome the ill-effects and learn well in school.

Thirty years ago, none of the students in my school were taking medications such as Ritalin and Prozac. Now, significant numbers of elementary students across America are being given medications such as these before school, during school and after school every weekday. Common sense would seem to suggest that some children who are experiencing the effects of these medications—as well as the underlying conditions that led to the prescription of the medications—might need additional learning time to do as well in school as the students who are drug-free and not suffering from the underlying conditions.

"According to the Drug Enforcement Administration, production of Ritalin has increased by nearly 500% in the last five years. Ritalin, like caffeine, diet pills, and the uppers some college students use to help themselves study, is a stimulant...Some children taking Ritalin complain of stomachaches or headaches, and many eat poorly...

Young children taking stimulant medications are also prone to be-coming moody, sad, irritable, or overly sedated and 'lifeless.'"

—*Early Childhood Today*, August/September, 1996.

This list could go on and on, but I hope the point is now clear and convincing. Today's educators are now seeing a wide range of new and complex student problems that were virtually or actually nonexistent just a few decades ago. That's why it is not uncommon to hear a veteran elementary school teacher say, "I used to be able to handle 30 kids, but not any more."

Before we give further consideration to the impact and consequences of these sorts of trends, however, we also need to consider another factor that has remained remarkably *unchanged* throughout recent decades.

Thirty years ago, a large number of students—sometimes as many as 20 to 30 percent—turned out to be "late bloomers." Some of these students had summer or fall birthdays and were therefore the youngest kids in the class, which meant they had significantly less time to develop and grow than the oldest kids in the class. Other children were *developmentally young*, which meant they were developing at a slower but still normal rate, and therefore were less well-prepared to succeed in school than children who were developing at a faster rate. A few children were both chronologically and developmentally young, which made them all the more likely to have problems learning when placed in a grade solely on the basis of their birthday.

"The younger children in any grade are far more likely than the older children in that grade to:

- *have failed a grade*
- *become dropouts*
- *be diagnosed as Learning Disabled*
- *be receiving various types of counseling services*
- *be behind their peers in athletic skill level*

- *be in special service programs such as Title I*
- *rank lower in their graduating class*
- *be a suicide victim*
- *be more of a follower than a leader*
- *be less attentive in class*
- *earn lower grades*
- *score lower on achievement tests."*

—*Real Facts from Real Schools* by James K. Uphoff, Ed.D.

"It would be a fallacy to think all children are ready at the same time. 'Late bloomers' deserve to be identified and have their pace respected."

—*Touchpoints* by T. Berry Brazelton, M.D.

In recent years, elementary school teachers continue to report similar percentages of students who are chronologically or developmentally young, and so are less ready to learn grade-level material. Common sense would seem to suggest that some children who are chronologically or developmentally young might need more time to develop and grow, in order to learn the same material as children who are older or developing faster. In fact, Dr. Uphoff's book shows that many late bloomers who received additional learning time ended up doing extremely well in school, while others who did not receive the additional time and support they needed ended up staying at the "bottom" of the class, and were more likely to be retained later in their school career.

Now, the percentage of late bloomers that has remained relatively constant has been combined with the percentage of "late learners" whose ability to succeed in school has been jeopardized by the range of other factors and circumstances described on the previous pages. We therefore have a much larger percentage of students who may need additional learning time. And, of course, some late bloomers are also experiencing the consequences of the other factors and circumstances, which leaves them even more adversely affected.

To put it more personally, what are the prospects for a left-handed boy with an August birthdate who was developing a bit more slowly than his peers, when all of a sudden his father loses his job and medical insurance? A change of address, an undetected or untreated ailment, emotional stress, physical abuse, malnutrition—could any or all of these make it even more difficult for this late bloomer to succeed in school? Is it fair or even rational to expect a child in this sort of situation to learn the same material at the same rate as a right-handed girl who is almost a full year older and comes from an emotionally and financially stable family? Is there really a "developmentally appropriate" curriculum that can be individualized to create a "level playing field" for both children, thereby enabling the boy to automatically catch up with the girl in third grade?

Get real.

Today's diverse and problem-ridden students need a range of educational programs that can effectively meet their needs and solve their problems. This includes not just a range of instructional methods and materials—and not just a range of ESL specialists, LD specialists, speech therapists, Title I teachers, resource room teachers, etc.—but also a range of time-flexibility options that enable students to master the curriculum and meet high standards no matter what their current developmental stage and individual learning rate.

When there's no time flexibility, some students are forced to try to learn to read and write before they are physically and intellectually ready to do so. And, some students are forced to absorb more and higher-level information than they are biologically ready to process. Then, when such totally inappropriate attempts at education fail to work as intended, these same students are forced to spend extensive amounts of time working with specialists or being subjected to intensive remediation, when all many of the students ever really needed was more time to develop and learn.

Today, most elementary schools recognize the importance of using a variety of teaching styles to match students' predominant *learning styles*, whether auditory, visual, tactile, or kinesthetic. Yet, many of these same schools absolutely refuse to acknowledge and accommodate different *learning rates*, even though the amount of time required to learn material can be just as important and variable as the way in which the material is learned.

> *"Research confirms common sense. Some students take three to six times longer than others to learn the same thing. Yet students are caught in a time trap—processed on an assembly line scheduled to the minute. Our usage of time virtually assures the failure of many students."*
>
> —Report of the National Education Commission on Time and Learning, 1994.

While a small group of education bureaucrats and ivory-tower academics has convinced some administrators that *all* students should be prohibited from having access to *any* extra-year options, most of the educators and parents who have firsthand experience with today's students recognize that for a variety of reasons, many students can *only* meet high standards and avoid being socially promoted if options that provide additional learning time—including retention—are available.

At this point, you may be wondering specifically how retention, which has been so vehemently condemned by the "ayatollahs of appropriate education," can actually help some of today's struggling students succeed in school? Let's consider a few possibilities.

For children who have been unable to learn grade-level material because their families are in crisis, another year in the same grade can provide extended time with a stable, caring, and valued adult, as well as additional time to learn information and skills that the children may have been too distracted and stressed to absorb the first time around.

For children who have been unable to learn grade-level material because they were still adjusting to a new school and community after frequent moves, another year in the same grade can postpone yet another important and disturbing change, as well as provide the additional time needed to learn methods and materials that were simply not taught at a previous school.

For children who have been unable to learn needed material because of frequent absences due to illness or other factors, another year in the same grade can provide the additional learning time such children often need to make up for the time in school that was lost through no fault of their own.

For children who have been unable to learn grade-level material due to their limited proficiency in the English language, another year in the same grade can provide extended time with someone who models spoken English appropriately and already understands the children's language and comprehension limitations. Retention can also provide the extra time needed to learn material that was literally incomprehensible one year earlier.

For children struggling to overcome the effects of exposure to drugs or environmental hazards that impede their ability to function—or for children struggling to live and work successfully with special needs— another year in the same grade can provide the additional time needed to help them overcome physical and emotional problems that interfered with the learning process and prevented them from learning grade-level material.

And, for children who happen to be chronologically or developmentally young, an extra year in the same grade can provide the additional time needed to develop and learn, so that these children—like all the others mentioned above—can experience and benefit from the advantages of being somewhat bigger instead of somewhat smaller, of feeling smarter instead of dumber, of leading more often than following, and of becoming a winner instead of a loser.

With so many different trends and factors undermining the education of so many different students in so many ways, only someone far-removed from the realities of today's classrooms could claim that *no* student should ever be provided with an extra year of school. Of course, it would be equally ridiculous to claim that *all* students in the categories listed above would benefit from retention. What is obviously needed is careful consideration of each student's individual needs, combined with a thorough understanding of a range of time-flexibility options that teachers and parents—not a few university professors and education bureaucrats—can select.

An effective response to today's student population would also include smaller class sizes and enhanced teacher training, as well as an increase in the social and medical services provided to children who are suffering from the sorts of problems described at the start of this chapter. But, as you probably know all too well, in many schools the class sizes are growing and teacher training is being cut, at the same time that children are receiving less access to social and medical services—all of which is likely to increase the number of children who need additional learning time.

And, with so many high-profile, desperately needy children to educate under such difficult circumstances, it's now even easier than ever to lose sight of the needs of a quiet, smart, healthy, well-mannered child who also would benefit from an extra year to develop and learn—not just academically but socially, emotionally, and physically, as well.

Keeping in the mind the diverse needs of today's students and the rigid structure of our old-fashioned school system, let's now take a look at what happens when today's "non-standard" kids and our highly standardized school system are not ready for each other.

Chapter 3

Ready Or Trouble

Once upon a time, when America's children and schools were in much better condition, the school year was filled with "Happy Days," and the students were treated as if they were "All in the Family."

Do you believe in fairy tales—or TV sit-coms?

If you're like most grown-ups, you probably know that both of these genres contain important elements of truth, even though many of their details are fictional. And, the same understanding should be applied to the statement at the start of this chapter.

Way back in the "good old days," our standardized school system did work more efficiently, because the "fit" between the kids and the schools was so much better. As explained in the last chapter, a far greater number of students came from intact, financially stable families in which neither the parents nor the children were on drugs—illegal or prescribed. The student population was far less mobile, almost entirely English speaking, and had no exposure whatsoever to cable TV, VCRs, video games, the Internet or other recent technological developments whose effects on young children are only beginning to be measured and understood.

At the same time, our schools were in better shape physically, teachers were respected rather than targeted, and the educational methods and materials being used were not divisive political issues. So, when kids from unified families and communities entered schools with

31

a unified curriculum, there were far fewer of the complex problems that now interfere with the education of today's children.

However, to maintain a comfortable fit, yesteryear's schools also used strategies and practices that are now widely considered unfair and counter-productive. In particular, rather than promoting the use of an individualized curriculum that meets the needs of diverse learners in an inclusive classroom, many schools relied on tracking and separate special education programs to "weed out" kids who didn't fit in a particular class. The kids placed in the "dummy" classes—whatever these classes were euphemistically named—usually knew exactly where they were and often acted accordingly, whatever their actual intelligence or potential. As a result, many late bloomers and other children whose initial difficulties could have been overcome ended up with bad attitudes and matching school records, which usually had a long-term, negative impact on their lives.

And, because both the school system and the student population were in better shape and more compatible with each other, it was far easier to "write off" kids who had serious problems in school as the few, defective products inevitably generated by any good factory. The dropout rate was higher in the 1950s and 1960s than in the 1990s, but the students who did graduate had skills that helped them find decent jobs, and even the drop-outs could often find "blue-collar" work that would keep them employed and out of trouble.

Now that the late bloomers have been joined by so many other children who have trouble learning within our standardized school system—substantially increasing the volume and complexity of the problems in our classrooms—the overall fit between the kids and the schools is far worse than it was in the past. Too many of today's kids are not "making the grade," and their problems in the classroom are having a very negative impact on other children in the class, which is now likely to include children with problems of their own that might have kept them out of such a class in the past.

Yet, our old-fashioned, standardized, lock-step school system still keeps trying to move all the students along the assembly line at the exact same rate. For despite the recent creation of all the magnet schools and model schools and charter schools and Edison schools, most of the educational reformers and their creations remain focused on the curriculum and methods of instruction, while leaving the same old time-bound, inflexible structure in place. And, the end result is the same old litany of education "crises," concerns, and criticism that we've all heard far too much of for far too many years.

"Decades of school improvement efforts have foundered on a fundamental design flaw, the assumption that learning can be doled out by the clock and defined by the calendar."

—*Report of the National Education Commission on Time and Learning,* 1994.

So, what can we do to solve the real, underlying problem, not just for the millions of young children across America, but also for a real, live, specific child that you just happen to know and care about and need to help *today?*

Well, according to some ivory-tower "experts," you should just do exactly what has been mandated by unknown state education bureaucrats, many of whom happen to belong to the same professional organizations and attend the same conferences as the "experts." They've already decided exactly what grade placement cut-off date and curriculum is appropriate for every child in your state. And, perhaps because these bureaucrats and their supporters are so busy talking with each other, they usually don't have much time to spend on any specific children, teachers, or parents who are encountering serious problems with the state-wide, "one-size-fits-all" plan.

Once the individual child's school readiness and grade placement have been determined solely on the basis of this totally impersonal and often impractical approach, the bureaucrats and "experts" then want you to make absolutely, positively sure the child is promoted along with his or her classmates for every remaining year of school, even if many classmates consider the child stupid and puny, and these classmates therefore like to mock the child in the classroom and beat up the child on the playground.

As I and too many other teachers, parents, and children have found, however, this approach actually causes and compounds many of today's education problems, rather than solving them. So, in order to find practical solutions that meet the real needs of individual children today, we must understand what *really* happens when this approach is used to force-feed today's non-standardized children into the old, inflexible, and highly standardized school systems still cranking along in communities across America.

The Readiness Dilemma

The most important element of the fit between a child and a school occurs right when a child first enters school. More than anything else, the initial placement of a child in a particular grade or program determines whether a child becomes comfortable, competent, and successful in school, or whether a child becomes unhappy, frustrated, and unsuccessful.

In some cases, initial difficulties can be overcome, and by the end of the year the child has found a place in the class and is doing well academically. In other cases, when the child has been placed in the wrong grade or program, the initial problems are never overcome during that crucial first year or in the years that follow.

"When children face a school environment that is too sophisticated and busy for their current stage of development, they start to see themselves as being incapable of doing anything right. This is where the pattern of failure begins, and it may never go away."

—*Starting School* by Judy Keshner.

Of course, virtually all children of school age are ready to learn something; the question is what they're ready to learn. When a school has a variety of grades or programs that meet different children's needs, those children are likely to be placed in a grade or program where they feel comfortable and are ready to succeed in school. But, when a variety of educational, financial, and ideological constraints combine to limit the options available to children, at least some children are likely to be placed in the *wrong* grade or program—one that does not meet their needs and so sets them up for failure instead of success.

As noted earlier, an understanding of *wrong grade placement* has been widespread since the 1960s, when Dr. Louise Bates Ames wrote her landmark article in *Reader's Digest*, "Is Your Child In The Wrong Grade." In that article and in a number of related books, Dr. Ames explained how children of the same chronological age can be developing at different but still normal rates, which can dramatically affect their school performance. Especially around the ages of 5 and 6, for example, some children are ready, willing, and able to work with a pencil and learn letters and numbers. Other children of the same chronological age might be ready to do the same things one year later, but if forced to try to do those things at the same time as children who are at a more advanced stage of development, the developmentally younger children are not only likely to fail, they are likely to "act out" and become disciplinary problems because they cannot learn successfully. They are then more likely to develop negative attitudes about school and themselves that can last a lifetime and prevent them from reaching their full potential.

Amazingly enough, these sorts of problems can become so severe that a developmentally young child may appear to have an Attention Deficit Disorder—or even be identified Learning Disabled and placed in a special education program—when, in fact, the child is really "curriculum-disabled" and could have succeeded in a regular program if given additional time to grow and learn. Of course, you may find it hard to believe that many of America's children are being incorrectly diagnosed and then mislabeled in this way, but if so, I'm afraid you haven't been keeping up with the news.

> *"Too many children are being identified as learning disabled and placed in special-education classrooms simply because they have trouble reading, according to a recent report from the International Reading Association. The term "learning disabled" has become too vague and has strayed from its original meaning, which referred to children with a neurological problem that has an academic component, the report says."*

—*Education Week*, September 27, 1995.

Further confirmation of the extent of the problem—and an effective solution—can be found in the book, *Real Facts from Real Schools*, by James Uphoff, Ed.D. This book contains summaries of numerous studies which show that programs providing additional learning time made students far less likely to be referred for special services. The following is just one such example, in which students who attended an extra-year Junior First Grade (JFG) between kindergarten and first grade were compared with students who were recommended for the program but whose parents sent them right into first grade instead:

> *"149 JFG students and 48 non-attending, but invited pupils were included in this part of the study. The results found that two years after eligibility, 11% of the JFG attendees were in Learning Disability (LD) programs, while 32% of the non-attendees were in LD programs. Four years after eligibility the two rates were 14% and 42% respectively."*

—*Real Facts from Real Schools* by James Uphoff, Ed.D., citing a study of the Sioux Falls, SD public schools.

In other words, three times as many students who did *not* receive an additional year of learning time ended up in Learning Disability programs. And, other studies comparing these sorts of children have found similar results.

Even when students remain in a regular classroom and are not officially mislabeled, a vicious cycle often develops in which academic problems lead to behavior problems which result in more academic problems, etc. It should therefore be no surprise that as extra-year options have been reduced or eliminated in recent years, educators across America have been struggling with a decrease in test scores—combined with an increase in disciplinary problems, special education referrals, and students suspected of having an Attention Deficit Disorder.

Given the critical importance of a child's readiness for school and initial grade placement, you might think that all schools would carefully evaluate the fit between the child and a particular grade or program. In fact, some public schools and many private schools do exactly that and then make grade placement decisions accordingly.

Unfortunately, most public schools continue to rely more on astrology than an understanding of children's different stages and rates of developments. In accordance with the proclamations of the unknown state bureaucrats and their "expert" supporters, too many schools rely solely on one arbitrary cut-off date, at which point all grade placement decisions are simply based on the number of candles on each child's most recent birthday cake, even though the problems with this approach have been obvious for decades.

Consider, for example, the fact that the school entrance cut-off dates vary from state to state, regardless of the difficulty of the curriculum. Most states use a cut-off date of August 31st or earlier, so that a child has to be 5 when he or she starts kindergarten. Yet, two of the nation's most populous states—California and New York—have December cut-off dates, which result in many of their kindergarten students being only 4-years-old for a significant portion of their first year of school. And, not only do California and New York *not* have a proportionately easier curriculum, in many locations they also have overcrowded classrooms filled with an especially diverse and needy student population, which can make teaching and learning all the more difficult.

This state-by-state approach also results in situations where a child living on one side of a state line has a full year more to grow and learn than a child born on the same day but living on the other side of a state line a few miles away. So, regardless of their individual needs and differences, one of the two children is allowed to develop and learn for an additional 365 days, which at that point equals just about 20% of the child's entire life.

And, even within the same state, a child who is developing at a slower rate and has numerous problems—but was born a day or two *before* the cut-off date—may be required to enter school, while a precocious child who is relatively problem-free and was born just *after* the cut-off date is supposed to grow and mature for another whole year before being asked to learn and do the same things. As a result, the following scenario is all too familiar to all too many teachers:

It's September, the start of the new school year in a district where the cut-off date for birthdays is September 1st and the first day of school is September 5th. Into a first grade classroom walks Prissie, who was born on September 2nd and is therefore the oldest child in the grade, having just turned 7. Prissie is also white, right-handed, well-behaved, and the daughter of middle-class parents. Her hobby is counting by threes, and in her spare time she likes to write stories with her unbitten pencil. All in all, Prissie is likely to do well in school and be easy to teach. In fact, if the teacher calls in sick, the principal can probably use Prissie instead of a substitute.

But, next to Prissie there's Skippy, who was born on August 31st at 11:59 PM and is therefore the youngest child in the grade, having just turned 6. Unknown state bureaucrats decided that Skippy should have 363 less days than Prissie to grow and learn before starting kindergarten, even though Skippy happens to be left-handed, was born two months premature, and—now that his parents are divorced—just moved to a small apartment which his mother has trouble affording even though she works full time. Unlike Prissie, Skippy likes to use pencils only as miniature javelins, and he has trouble even listening to stories, much less writing them. His main function in school seems to be giving the principal something to do. And, it's a good thing Prissie can act as a substitute teacher, because all of the grown-up substitutes who filled in for Skippy's kindergarten teacher last year refuse to go back to any classroom that's supposed to contain him.

So, even though Prissie and Skippy aren't really the same chronological age or at the same developmental stage, the unknown state bureaucrats and "experts" insist that these two children must be kept together until they graduate from high school, supposedly so that Skippy will have lots of self-esteem and a positive attitude about school. But, as should be obvious to anyone who deals with actual children instead of statistics, continuing to place and keep Skippy in grades for which he is not yet ready is far more likely to make him think he's a stupid trouble-maker who is much happier when he's not in school— all of which makes getting suspended and dropping out of school at an early age very logical and attractive goals for him.

Meanwhile, Prissie's and Skippy's poor first grade teacher has been told that if she just individualizes the curriculum and uses "developmentally appropriate practices," Skippy won't need any additional time to grow and learn. But, hard as she tries to be totally appropriate and meet Skippy's individual needs—along with those of all the other children in the class—Prissie and Skippy are still looking at each other across the same great divide in June, when they both are automatically deemed ready for second grade, even though Skippy can only read a few sight words and Prissie can read chapter books. The first grade teacher comforts herself with the knowledge that some "experts" claim Skippy will automatically catch up with Prissie in grade 3, but the teacher knows she can't mention that to the second and third grade teachers—who have never, ever seen that happen in all their years of teaching, and who blame the first grade teacher for not having "jump-started" Skippy's reading, writing, and arithmetic.

Is this any way to run a school system? I sure don't think so. And, neither do many other educators and parents who have firsthand experience with today's schools and children.

> *"Incorrect grade placement has also caused the needless destruction of eager, intelligent, potentially successful children whose start of schooling (and choice of grade level) is governed purely by their birthdates and their school's cut-off policies. Many of these children are boys, many have summer birthdays. Many have been brutally injured by adults' automatic adherence to numbers of calendars."*
>
> —*Emotion: The On/Off Switch for Learning* by Priscilla Vail.

The not-so-funny thing is that despite the obvious flaws of this approach, some bureaucrats and "experts" not only insist it's the one and only way to go, they actively fight any attempts to provide any children with additional time to grow and learn. For example, in 1989 a few college professors and state officials associated with National Association for the Education of Young Children (NAEYC) were at the forefront of an effort to ban extra-year programs for young children in Texas. And, a few years later people representing the Ohio branch of the same organization opposed moving back the state's school entrance cut-off date from September until July, which would have provided an additional year to learn and grow for the "summer children" whose July and August birthdates traditionally made them the youngest students in a grade and the ones most likely to have trouble in it. As you might expect, people linked to the same organization have also been trying to prohibit retention in schools across America.

Why devote time, energy, and money to preventing young children from having additional time to grow and learn? Here's how one NAEYC member summarizes the organization's thinking:

"NAEYC argues that schools should change so children do not need extra time in order to succeed. They have proposed a shift toward more developmentally appropriate practices in kindergarten and in the primary grades as a way of reducing the large number of children deemed to be unready for school. In a NAEYC publication titled, Kindergarten Policies: What Is Best For Children, co-author Joanne Peck states that instead of increasing the age of school entry, 're-sources and energy should instead be redirected to offering a good program.' Many supporters of this position feel that [extra-time] programs impede progress toward the goal of creating developmentally appropriate curriculums for all students."

—*What's Best For Kids* by Anthony Coletta, Ph.D.

As with the timebound approach itself, there are also a number of fairly obvious flaws with these arguments, some of which Dr. Coletta proceeds to explain in his book. (In fact, I have found that many NAEYC members disagree with these arguments, which have been promoted mainly by the national and state leaders of the organization. And, it should be noted that NAEYC is primarily an organization of daycare providers and preschool teachers. Very few elementary school teachers I speak with are members.)

Nevertheless, many elementary school educators have tried using "developmentally appropriate practices" to reduce the number of children who are not yet ready to succeed in a particular grade or program. However, these practices were rigidly defined by "experts" who apparently believed that only they knew what was best for children they did not personally know. And, until recently, their pronouncements have been interpreted by many educators to mean that primary grade students should not be taught to use rote memorization and correct spelling, and that the curriculum should be de-escalated (sometimes referred to as "dumbed down") so that it could match the abilities of the least able kids in the class.

As should now be abundantly clear, a great many parents, educators, politicians, and pundits believe otherwise—rightly or wrongly. And, now that this approach has been subjected to widespread attacks, the organization that originally defined these practices has found it necessary to issue a "revamped position statement."

> *"The statement is designed, in part, to address what NAEYC officials consider to be misinterpretations of their previously published lists of developmentally appropriate and inappropriate practices... The old list of practices was 'never meant to be a cookbook,' even though that was how it was used, particularly by novices in the field who might not have had a background in child development, Ms. Willer [an NAEYC spokesperson], said."*

—*Education Week*, November 27, 1996.

To many educators now under intense pressure to teach basic skills and maintain high standards in their schools, the varying official pronouncements about developmentally appropriate practices have become increasingly irrelevant. Still, I continue to encounter puzzled educators who report that they have made their classrooms "developmentally appropriate" and refuse to provide any extra-year options, but somehow many of their students did not catch up with their classmates and are not ready to succeed in the upper grades.

These educators and their students are learning the hard way that focusing only on the curriculum and related instructional practices is an academic approach that does not address two crucial aspects of the learning process—each child's current stage and rate of development. As noted earlier, these individual characteristics are determined by a unique combination of biological and environmental factors and circumstances, which vary widely among children of about the same chronological age. No curriculum and method of instruction has ever been proven to overcome all these individual differences and enable the full range of children in a grade to learn the same material at the same rate—or even within the same timeframe.

In addition, because the intellectual, physical, and social/emotional aspects of development all affect a child's success in school, there can also be wide variations in the different aspects of a child's overall development—which the curriculum cannot affect, but which do affect the learning of the curriculum. One common example of this phenomenon is a child who is bright but small, as well as socially and emotionally immature. This sort of child often does well academically at first, but has trouble making friends and enjoying school. In many cases, this later leads to social and emotional problems—and a lack of interest in school—which sabotage the child's academic performance just when it becomes increasingly important for the child's future success.

This sort of variation in children's developmental readiness, combined with the different learning rates and all the other factors and circumstances that affect a child's academic performance, make extra-year options essential to the success of a *truly* "developmentally appropriate curriculum," rather than something that "impedes progress" towards it. Unfortunately, in many states there is continued pressure on educators to withhold additional learning time from children who need it, while efforts to "fix" the non-standardized kids and our highly standardized school system continue.

This is especially troubling when so many children have been shown *not* to be ready to succeed in the grade or program in which they have been placed. While teachers and parents have been well aware of this problem for decades, only in the early 1990s did it receive national and official recognition, based in large part on surveys documenting the extent of the problem.

"Frankly, we found it deeply troubling, ominous really, that 35% of the nation's children—more than one in three—are not ready for school, according to the teachers. Even more disturbing, when we asked how the readiness of last year's students compared to those

who enrolled five years ago, 42 percent of the respondents said the situation is getting worse; only 25 percent said it's better."

—*Ready To Learn* by Ernest Boyer, citing a 1991 survey conducted by The Carnegie Foundation for the Advancement of Teaching.

"Students are not fully prepared to learn at their grade level...55% of teachers report that all, most or at least more than one-quarter of their students are unprepared...It should be noted that lack of preparedness is a problem at all grade levels."

—1992 Metropolitan Life Survey of the American Teacher.

The Readiness Goal

In response to this and other data, then-President George Bush and the nation's governors established a set of education goals for the year 2000, starting with a readiness goal—that all children will start school "ready to learn." In order to achieve this goal, ambitious plans were made to provide more extensive and better pre-natal and post-natal care for children, improved nutrition, and increased access to Head Start and preschool.

Of course, actually implementing these plans would have required massive spending increases, major improvements in the way health care is provided to low-income families, and continued bi-partisan support for the Goals 2000 program—none of which actually occurred. Instead, many young children continued to receive inadequate health care, poor nutrition, and little or no appropriate education prior to starting kindergarten, with thoroughly predictable results. Five years after the Goals 2000 program began to take shape—and half-way to the year in which the Goals were supposed to be reached—reports continued to find that almost the exact same percentage of students were not ready to learn and succeed in school.

"As many as one-third of American students entering the K-12 system need extra help to keep up with their peers, the [Years of Promise] report says."

—*Education Week,* September 18, 1996, citing a 1996 report by the Carnegie Corporation of New York.

While the Goals 2000 program probably would have helped to *reduce* the number of children who are *not* starting school ready to learn successfully, it could not have eliminated the readiness dilemma even if the program had been fully funded and implemented. One reason is that it did not address the dilemma of developmentally young children—whose rate of development cannot be sped up by good health care, nutrition, and preschools. Many late bloomers come from emotionally and financially stable families which provide these prerequisites but still find that the children need additional time to grow and learn before they are ready to succeed in school.

Another crucial limitation of the Goals 2000 program is that it totally ignored the dilemma of all the children who were already entering America's elementary schools before the readiness goal was achieved. These children—who had been clearly identified as *not* ready to learn and succeed in school—were simply left to flounder and fail within the nation's elementary schools, unless the schools could come up with their own innovative programs to save such unfortunate children. And, as the readiness goal has not been and probably never will be reached, each year many children are continuing to enter school and be placed in grades or program for which they are not yet ready, leaving America's educators and parents with the responsibility of deciding for themselves how best to handle this difficult and unrelenting problem for individual children *now*.

In order to truly solve the readiness dilemma of *today's* elementary school students, therefore, factors such as the developmental stage and learning rate of the individual child must be weighed against the specific curriculum and options available within the school that the child is actually attending. The top-down, one-size-fits-all approach never has and never can succeed in meeting the needs of the individual children in different schools in just one state, much less all across America.

The only practical way to meet those needs is also the right way—by making informed decisions about individual children, and making sure there are time-flexibility options available that meet different children's needs. For if there are no such options available at all, then many children will continue to be socially promoted year after year, even though they are actually *failing* to learn needed material, meet high standards, and succeed in other ways, as well. Or, if the only option that provides additional learning time is retention, some children will need to be socially promoted because retention is not a viable option for them, and other children will suffer needlessly and still not succeed in school because retention was not really the best choice for them.

But, when schools provide a range of options right from the start of a child's school career—including readiness classes before kindergarten, continuous-progress transition classes between grades, multiage classes in which children can remain an extra year, and different ways in which retention can be implemented—then schools are truly ready for their students and can meet the different needs of different students. These are the options which provide educators and parents with real choices for the children in their care, and which have actually been implemented successfully in schools across America. These are also the options that we'll now proceed to examine in the chapters that follow.

Chapter 4

Retention Prevention Through Extra-Time Intervention & Same-Grade Accommodation

You may not consider the 1970s and 1980s the "good old days," but for many late bloomers and late learners—and their parents and teachers—that's exactly what those decades were.

Way back then, many public schools had continuous-progress classes that provided an additional year of learning time either before kindergarten or after kindergarten. These classes—often called readiness or transition classes—provided late bloomers and other children with the additional time they needed to learn and succeed right when they were first starting school, before they were locked into a rigid grade structure, allowed to struggle and fail, and then either retained or socially promoted.

Research compiled about schools that offered such programs showed that many of them produced very positive results in regard to academic achievement, social and emotional benefits, and parent and teacher satisfaction. This data includes independent, longitudinal studies which followed the "graduates" of such programs into middle school and beyond. Numerous studies also found that "control groups" of students who were recommended for the programs but did not participate had high rates of upper-grade retention, as well as other problems.

"The high quality of these studies makes their results all the more important, and the results clearly show that school readiness programs remain needed, widespread, popular, and successful alternatives to retention."

—*Real Facts from Real Schools* by James Uphoff, Ed.D.

As noted earlier in this book, however, a series of articles in the late 1980s began attacking these programs and the use of retention. A small group of university professors and education bureaucrats—along with a spokesperson for the National Association for the Education of Young Children—appeared in article after article, proclaiming the availability of any extra-year options to be "inappropriate," and instead promoting the use of the "developmentally appropriate practices" championed by NAEYC.

As documented by Dr. Uphoff, this negative media campaign failed to prove either that extra-year programs were unsuccessful or that developmentally appropriate practices were successful. Yet, the campaign did succeed in providing some administrators with an excuse to eliminate local programs and achieve some short-term budgetary savings, even though the flaws in the negative arguments and data quickly became apparent, as did the resulting problems for students.

"The 'research' still being used by critics is based on purportedly negative data about extra-year programs, rather than positive data proving that the alleged alternatives to extra-year programs actually work ."

—*Real Facts from Real Schools* by James Uphoff, Ed.D.

As I and many other educators had predicted, many of the administrators who eliminated their readiness and transition classes quickly began to find that the resulting increases in referrals for support ser-vices and special education—as well as the resulting increases in up-per-grade retentions—created even greater budgetary pressures and also worked *less* well for many of the unfortunate students who were unnecessarily subjected to them.

So, now that these pressures and the need for higher standards in our schools have combined to create renewed interest in retention and its prevention, we need to look once again at the extra-time options which were developed specifically as alternatives to retention, and which have been proven in numerous schools to work well as such. In addition, we also need to consider other alternatives which do not pro-vide an additional year of learning time but which may help some stu-dents who are at-risk of being retained solely for *academic* reasons. This is an important distinction, because children who truly need an addi-tional year to learn and grow—rather than help with one or two sub-jects areas—should not be offered ineffective substitutes, especially when there is such widespread, authoritative support for providing additional learning time to children who need it.

> *"As decisions about preschool, kindergarten, and first grade arise, the following reasons to give children extra time should be considered:*
>
> *Family patterns of slow development—'late bloomers'*
>
> *Prematurity or physical problems in early life*
>
> *Immature motor development—awkwardness, poor motor skills, such as in catching or throwing a ball, drawing, or cutting*
>
> *Easy distractibility or short attention span*
>
> *Difficulty with right-left hand or eye-hand coordination, such as in copying a circle or diamond*
>
> *Lagging social development—difficulty taking turns, sharing, or playing. If the child is shunned by children her own age, take it seri-ously.*

Each of these might be a reason to allow a child to mature another year before starting preschool, or to stay in preschool or kindergarten a year longer."

—*Touchpoints* by T. Berry Brazelton, M.D.

Extra-Time Intervention

Early intervention is recognized in many fields as a vital way of preventing later problems. This holds true in education and is one of the main reasons for the success and popularity of programs that provide additional time to grow and learn during the early childhood years. Rather than waiting until a child has experienced years of frustration and failure, and then providing the additional time that the child needed all along, the extra-time interventions described in this section of the chapter provide a child with appropriate educational experiences that allow a child to succeed in school right from the beginning. Children in these programs can build a solid foundation of knowledge and skills that will lead to continued success, while also developing a positive attitude about school and themselves that supports the learning process.

High-quality preschool or primary grade programs that offer additional learning time have many different names, but they share a number of important features, such as reasonable class sizes, a rich assortment of educational resources, and a room with space for movement. Children in these programs learn social skills, practice listening and speaking, develop their physical capabilities, gain experience with different types of literature, work with hands-on math and science materials, explore the creative arts, and improve their problem-solving abilities. These sorts of developmentally appropriate activities provide young children with vital information and skills.

The selection and placement of children in these extra-time programs should be based on multiple sources of information. Developmental assessments or school readiness screening devices can help to determine the child's current stage of development, by evaluating such factors as the child's motor skills, coordination, attention span, visual perception, clarity of speech, ability to follow directions, and ability to sustain a function—all important elements of school success in the primary grades. This sort of data should always be combined with other information based on parents' and teachers' observations. Parents can provide vital information about a child's background and current experiences outside of school, while teachers can provide a needed perspective based on their years of experience observing children in group situations, as well as their firsthand knowledge of whatever educational programs are available.

Many schools have a range of time-flexibility options available to meet the different needs of individual children, and if I were the superintendent of the universe—or even one school district—I would want my schools to offer a number of the programs described below.

Readiness Classes For "Young 5's"

As documented in the previous chapter, kindergarten teachers across America continue to find that as many as one-third of the incoming children are not ready to succeed in kindergarten. Rather than just blaming the kindergarten curriculum and teachers for this problem, we need to remember that more than a few of today's children have been "warehoused" in low-quality, high-volume day care centers—or in front of television sets at home—without ever having been taught such basic information and skills as the names of colors and the days of the week, how to use crayons and take turns, or how to talk politely with adults and follow their instructions. Other late bloomers and late learners who have been taught such basic information and skills may still need additional time to mature—due to the variety of factors and circumstances described earlier—before they can participate successfully in group and individual learning activities for a reasonable period of time.

So, instead of insisting that the curriculum be adjusted downward until it reaches the level of the least able members of each class—who are still likely to need an inordinate amount of the teacher's time and thereby deprive their classmates of the support and instruction they deserve—many schools provide an extra year to learn and grow in a supportive educational environment before children start kindergarten. This makes kindergarten a much more productive and positive experience for all students. And, it is especially important for the children who need more time to master needed information and skills, because as veteran kindergarten teacher Judy Keshner explains in her booklet, *Starting School*, "kindergarten is not a preview of what is to come—it is the foundation on which the following years will grow. Each grade builds on the one that came before, and kindergarten sets the pattern and the tone."

By providing additional learning time when a child first enters school, readiness classes enable late bloomers and late learners to experience success and develop positive attitudes right from the start of their elementary school experience. In addition, research studies have shown that these sorts of readiness classes help to reduce the likelihood of a variety of later problems, including retention. For example, consider the following data from a study which compared students who attended an "Early Fives" (E5's) readiness class to students who were recommended for the program but did not participate (NE5's).

"...the report also found that 43 (37%) of the 115 unmatched Comparison (NE5) students had been held back for a year sometime later in their school career, whereas only 4 (2%) of the 136 E5's took [a standardized achievement test] a year later than expected. Receiving remedial center help was an intervention used by 26 of 73 matched NE5's but only 13 of their E5 counterparts. Thus, twice as many NE5's needed remedial assistance."

—Real Facts from Real Schools by James Uphoff, Ed.D., citing an independent research study of the Farmington, MI public schools.

Transition Classes

These extra-year options provide an additional year to learn and grow in between two grades—usually between kindergarten and first grade. Obviously, this is very different than retention, not only in that the students have a new, continuous-progress curriculum in a different classroom with a different teacher, but also in that their classmates are other children of about the same age who were with them in kindergarten and moved along with them to the transition class.

Transition classes can be particularly valuable for kindergartners who are not yet ready to switch from the play-oriented learning of kindergarten to the more formal "academic tasks" which become increasingly important in first grade. Many schools consider first grade the year in which students learn to read and write, and first graders who need more time before trying to achieve this very difficult and crucial goal are likely to suffer many short-term and long-term consequences as a result of being pushed to do too much too soon. Not only can a transition class provide additional, needed instruction in pre-literacy skills, it can also provide time for the biological growth that some students need to develop the fine-motor skills and hand-eye coordination that are vital elements of successful reading and writing.

Now that strict standards are being used in many schools to determine whether children can proceed to the next grade, upper-grade transition classes may also prove helpful between grades such as 3 and 4, when the emphasis switches from "learning to read" to "reading to learn." If students are required to pass a standardized test at such a point in order to proceed to the next grade, many schools are likely to find that large numbers of their students cannot be promoted each year, at which point a "half-step" transition class which provides a continuous-progress instruction for chronological peers in a supportive environment could be a preferable alternative to retention. The data compiled on numerous K-1 transition classes, such as the summary of an official school district study shown below, clearly supports this sort of approach.

"SUMMARY

1. Children attending TK-1 [a transition class] are NOT put at risk for academic, social, emotional, or attendance difficulties later on. A survey of students referred to At-Risk Counselors at the Junior High level revealed that NOT ONE of the referred students had attended TK-1.

2. TK-1 students performed better in the classroom and on standardized achievement tests than did the students who were recommended for TK-1 but promoted to first grade at the parents' request.

3. Parents of children who attended TK-1 report that their children were happy when attending TK-1 and continue to be happy students with positive self-concepts as third graders.

4. Principals report that parents of TK-1 students and the community as a whole are pleased with the TK-1 program.

5. Principals report fewer discipline problems since the TK-1 programs have been implemented."

—Fayetteville, NC "Developmental Placement Program Study," cited in *Real Facts from Real Schools* by James Uphoff, Ed.D.

Multiage Primary Classes

A growing number of schools now offer classes in which children of different ages work and learn together with the same teacher for more than one year. These classrooms eliminate the artificial time constraints created by having separate primary grades, which result in high-stakes grade placement decisions and high-pressure, time-constrained instructional plans.

Multiage classes also offer an important advantage in that more time is available for teaching and learning, especially at the start of the school year, because the teacher and students don't have to spend time getting to know one another and learning to work well together. These classes also reduce worries about "running out of time" to complete the curriculum by the end of each year. Children can simply pick up where they left off when they return in the fall, and if at the end of the program a child still needs additional time to complete the curriculum before moving on, a multiage classroom can be a particularly hospitable place to spend an extra year, because it already contains a wide range of age levels and a flexible timetable, rather than a rigid, lockstep grade structure.

This developmental diversity also makes it easier for transfer and special-needs students to be included in a multiage classroom. And, staying in the same class with the same teacher and classmates for more than one year provides a sense of consistency and belonging, which can be particularly helpful for the many children who now grow up in fast-changing families and communities. Most of all, allowing all the students to develop and learn at their own rate in a much less hurried environment decreases their risk of failure and increases their enjoyment of learning and school, as the following excerpts from a report on a two-year multiage class indicate:

> "We feel that our move to Multiage has been successful for students, parents and ourselves. Our program offers continuous progress for all students in a natural setting. Our waiting list grows with each passing year. Parental responses to program evaluations done yearly are positive. We love what we are doing and most important, the students love coming to school!"

—Report on the Bucksport, ME Multiage Primary Class by Karin McKeen and Chris O'Roak.

Looping

Looping is the practice of allowing a teacher to work with the same students over a two-year period or even longer. For example, the teacher of a kindergarten class might also teach the same students in first grade and beyond. While this increasingly popular practice does not provide an additional year of growing and learning time, it does provide additional instructional time by eliminating the "getting-to-know-you" period at the beginning of the second year of a looping class. Students pick up where they left off at the end of the previous year, both instructionally and socially, and this can save as much as a month or more of time that is usually spent on evaluation and transition rather than instruction.

As with a multiage classroom, looping allows a teacher to work in a more sustained way with students' learning styles and individual needs. And, the students have more time with a consistent and caring role model who is attuned to them. This extended time together builds deeper bonds between the students and teacher, which can support and facilitate the learning process. Research from a district which uses this approach throughout grades 1-8 shows that it provides important benefits:

> "Student attendance in grades 2 through 8 has been increased from 92 percent average daily attendance (ADA) rate to 97.2 percent ADA. Retention rates have decreased by over 43 percent in those same grades. Discipline and suspensions, especially at the middle schools (grades 5 through 8), have declined significantly. Special education referrals have decreased by over 55 percent..."

—Report by Dr. Joseph Rappa, superintendent of the Attleboro, MA school district, cited in *The Looping Handbook* by Jim Grant, Bob Johnson, and Irv Richardson.

Summer School & Other Schedule Adjustments

Summer school, extended school days, or supplemental courses paid for privately are all ways of providing additional instructional time, and so can be of help to students who need more time to study and learn specific information and skills. What these sorts of options cannot do is provide the additional time to develop that a child may need in order to learn specific information and skills successfully.

Wishful thinking sometimes leads parents and educators to hope that two months of additional work will solve the problems of a child who is six or nine months behind his classmates developmentally or academically. Unfortunately, no one has yet invented a product like Miracle-Gro for children, so none of the many children I've known or taught have ever experienced more than two months of growth in two months. While growth spurts do occur, the other children in a class also continue to grow during the same timeframe, and they may have their own spurts during that or some other time. Extended instructional time may therefore help a developmentally young student in some respects, but it is not an effective substitute for an extra year to learn and grow in a supportive educational environment.

Parents, in particular, also need to remember the importance of physical, social, and emotional development, all of which support academic achievement. A child who is constantly deprived of opportunities for physical activity and creative play is likely to develop other problems—including a negative attitude—that can undermine whatever academic achievement does occur during extended school days or school years.

An Additional Year To Grow & Learn Before School

Especially when elementary schools do not offer options that provide additional learning time, allowing late bloomers and late learners to spend an extra year in preschool can be a very positive alternative to sending them off to kindergarten and waiting to find out whether they will "sink or swim." An extra year to grow and learn in a supportive preschool environment can greatly decrease the odds that a child will flounder and need rescuing in the primary grades.

High-quality preschools provide children with a range of developmentally appropriate activities that support the learning process. And, the mixed age levels in most preschools make it easy for slightly older children to fit in. This sort of environment tends to make preschool teachers focused on readiness and adept at working with children who are at various developmental levels.

Unfortunately, access to any preschool—much less an extra year of it—is usually available only to the children of financially advantaged parents. As a result, the failure of public schools to provide time-flexibility options puts financially disadvantaged children at an even greater risk, because they have not had the preschool experiences or additional learning time that could help them avoid being retained or socially promoted in elementary school.

Head Start was developed to help these sorts of children, but it has never been fully funded and so is not available to many of them. Now, however, a growing number of elementary schools have started their own programs for 4-year-olds. Like Head Start, these programs can help many young, at-risk children overcome knowledge-based deficiencies by providing language enrichment and supporting the development of readiness and social skills. And, by also providing other essential services such as free or reduced price lunches, they can help to prevent physical problems that might otherwise develop and interfere with the learning process. While these programs, like Head Start, tend to have limited availability and were not set up to provide an additional year of learning and growing time for older children, they could prove to be a viable time-flexibility option.

Some parents may prefer to provide late bloomers or late learners with an additional year to learn and grow at home. When a parent can afford to stay at home and has the time, inclination, and understanding needed to work with a child on readiness skills, this can be a viable alternative, especially now that more materials and support networks have been developed for parents who opt to "home school" their children. Some proponents of this approach also support it because it should enable a child to stay with the same class throughout all the years of school, and thus avoid being officially labeled as someone who was retained or placed in an extra-year program.

In many cases, parents can simply notify the local public school of their intent and send children to kindergarten one year later. However, young children need opportunities to grow and learn with other children. This helps prepare them to succeed in school and contributes to their overall development in other ways, as well. In addition, well-trained preschool and elementary school teachers can often provide a wider range of supportive and educational learning experiences than a parent can. But, if additional learning time for a child in need cannot be arranged at a local preschool or elementary school, the child may be better off growing and learning happily at home than floundering and failing in a kindergarten class for which the child is not yet ready.

Retention Prevention through Same-Grade Accommodation

Once a child has been placed in the wrong grade, retention prevention is a far more difficult challenge. There is simply no way to fast-forward the development of a late bloomer who is not yet ready to succeed in a particular grade. And, when late learners have multiple co-occurring factors and circumstances that prevent them from succeeding in a particular grade, school officials usually have a very limited ability to untangle the web of problems that extend outside the school but directly affect what happens in the classroom.

Nevertheless, there are programs and services that have been promoted as viable alternatives to retention, and they deserve careful evaluation when considered for this purpose. Following is a brief summary of some of the benefits and limitations of these proposed alternatives.

Specialized Reading Programs

Intensive, direct instruction in reading can help struggling students in schools where they may become candidates for retention *solely* because they are having difficulty learning to read. This sort of academic retention rarely works well and is not something I would recommend, but it may become more common in schools which have strict standards and promotion requirements in *one* specific subject area. In most cases, however, children who become candidates for retention are having difficulty with a number of different subject areas—not just reading—and common sense would seem to suggest that an intensive reading program would not solve all the problems of a child who is also having trouble with arithmetic, science, and social studies.

Yet, some "experts" are touting extremely expensive, specialized reading programs as an all-around alternative to retention, even though these programs have a limited focus and are also likely to have limited availability, because of their expense to the school system and their requirements for admission. One of the best known programs of this sort can only be used in first grade and does *not* accept students whose records show high absenteeism, frequent changes of address, an extra year of learning time, learning disabilities, or other multiple, complex needs. Obviously, a program with these sorts of extensive limitations deliberately excludes a high proportion of the students who are likely to need additional learning time—or even just help with reading. So, its value just as a reading program, much less an effective alternative to retention, needs very careful consideration.

Remedial & Support Services

Many schools now offer a wide array of services to struggling students, and many of these services do help children overcome specific problems. Students may receive additional assistance from a reading specialist, a speech and language therapist, a Title I math or language teacher, a learning disability or other special education teacher, an occupational therapist, a social worker, or some combination of the above. In addition, peer tutors, older students, and private tutors may also be available to help.

As long as a child is truly capable of doing grade-level work, this sort of assistance can help the child make up for deficits or gain the knowledge and skills that will enable the child to succeed in particular subject areas. When children are late bloomers or late learners, however, they may be intellectually and even physically incapable of doing required work until further growth and learning occur. In this sort of situation, the time spent on additional assistance is not only wasted because it does not meet the child's true needs, it also further reinforces the sense of frustration and failure that a struggling learner is already experiencing. Late bloomers, in particular, are likely to feel that if they cannot succeed even with all the extra effort and assistance, they must just be very stupid and unable to succeed no matter how hard they try.

Even when children could benefit from remedial and support services, it is also quite possible that the needed services will not be available. Not all schools offer a full range of support services, and many that do offer such services find that the growing numbers of students in need of assistance far surpass the availability of support personnel. It is not at all uncommon for specialists to become "booked" very early in the school year and then remain unavailable to help students whose problems occur or become apparent a few months later. Other students may find that they do not "qualify" for special assistance because of their income level or because their diagnosis does not fit established categories. This has become so common that the term "gray-area kids" is now widely used to describe students whose problems are not easily identified or remediated but still interfere with the learning process.

Rather than promoting these sorts of services as a panacea, therefore, their effectiveness as alternatives to retention must be evaluated very carefully in regard to their actual availability and their potential for solving both the apparent and underlying problems of individual students.

"Developmentally Appropriate Practices"

As noted elsewhere in this book and throughout the media campaigns unleashed on educators and parents during the early 1990s, members of the National Association for the Education of Young Children have promoted the idea that the use of their "Developmentally Appropriate Practices" (DAP) can eliminate the need for any extra-year programs in elementary schools, including retention. As of the writing of this book, however—close to ten years after these claims first began to appear—I still have not seen even *one* single study showing that this has really occurred at even *one* actual elementary school, much less at the multitude of schools which have compiled valid, longitudinal data on the success of students who participated in readiness and transition programs.

In addition, the promotion of DAP of as an alternative to retention and other extra-year programs is suspect because of the growing criticism of DAP, which was also promoted as an alternative to the more traditional teaching practices condemned as "inappropriate" for the primary grades by zealous DAP supporters. The NAEYC's "revamped position statement" has not satisfied all these critics, who still disagree with its overall approach to early childhood education.

> "Schoolwork that has been called 'developmentally inappropriate' has been proved to be highly appropriate to millions of students the world over, while the infantile pabulum now fed to American children is developmentally inappropriate (in a downward direction) and often bores them."
>
> —The Schools We Need & Why We Don't Have Them by E.D. Hirsch, Jr.

Common sense would seem to suggest that prohibiting traditional teaching practices and any extra-year options would, in fact, lead to the forced social promotion and upper-grade retention of at least some students who lack needed knowledge and skills. And, that is exactly what has occurred in many schools which relied on DAP and the hope that students would all "catch up" with each other in third grade.

In the light of what appear to be some fairly obvious flaws with this approach, as well as a total lack of supporting evidence for claims that it will eliminate the need for an additional year of learning time, I hope it will not be a big surprise when I state that I do *not* consider DAP alone to be an effective means of retention prevention.

Weighing the Options

Faced with difficult circumstances and intense pressures, many concerned educators and parents may want the best of both worlds—extra time and support services for struggling students. Of course, this would be the best solution for a child who truly needs both. There's certainly no reason whatsoever to deny support services to a child who is receiving or has received additional time to learn and grow, as time-flexibility options have been shown to *reduce*—not *eliminate*—the percentage of children who need such services. Virtually all educators and parents who believe in providing additional learning time also believe in providing support services to children who need those services. Unfortunately, not all adults who believe in providing support services also believe in providing additional learning time to children who need that time.

As noted in some of the studies cited earlier, there are almost always some parents who decline to provide their children with additional learning time, even when high-quality extra-year programs are available and recommended. Many of these children end up receiving extensive support services, which may prop them up enough to continue progressing from grade to grade, without enabling them to become truly successful and enthusiastic learners. A few may make an unexpected breakthrough, but most such students are far more likely to become candidates for retention at a later and more disruptive stage of their education. In the meantime, they will probably just keep "scraping by" unhappily from year to year, without the "margin of error" that would enable them to overcome a severely traumatic event—like a long illness or a family break-up—which might have such a negative impact that promotion to the next grade would no longer be feasible.

Other struggling learners may be in the even more unfortunate situation of having no options available. A school may offer none of the extra-time interventions described above, and have severely limited support services for which a particular child does not qualify. A student in this situation who is struggling and failing due to wrong grade placement must then be socially promoted without having succeeded in learning needed material, or be retained so that he or she can have additional time to prepare for the next grade.

In this and other situations, retention can be a positive extra-time intervention that leads to school success. Whether it is one of several options that provide additional learning time or it is the only way to obtain such time, it should be considered as a means of achieving the right fit between an individual student and the particular school that child is attending. The following chapter explains how to make this sort of evaluation.

Chapter 5

Ready For A High-Stakes Decision?

Way back when, students who had not learned what they were supposed to learn—or just flunked too many tests—were often "held back" for those reasons alone. If another year in the same grade did not result in a substantial improvement, the child was likely to be retained again—and again and again and again, for as long as the stalemate continued. Of course, after a few years of continued frustration, embarrassment, and failure, a child was far more likely to drop out of school than to keep coming back for more.

By the time I started teaching in the late 1960s, many educators had learned to base retention decisions on more than just academic performance. These educators usually considered a student's report card and ability to function in class, in combination with at least some information about the child's emotional, social, and physical development. And, wise educators also talked with the parents and took their views into account. Although schools could—and, in some cases, did—require a child to repeat a grade, experienced educators knew that allowing parents to make the final decision was often the best way to proceed for all concerned.

Now, we have even more data and experience to help us evaluate the many factors and circumstances that can influence a retention decision and its results. Educators like myself have had decades to study and re-evaluate the development of children who received additional learning time, as well as children who might have benefited from this sort of early intervention but did not receive it. This knowledge has confirmed the importance of considering the full range of factors and circumstances that have led a child to become a candidate for retention and that may continue affecting the child after a decision has been made.

> *"Children who do not keep exact pace are not labeled failures; a vigorous effort is made to learn why that child seems laggard and to correct the situation.*
>
> *If retention is considered, the decision is never based on a single factor but on a variety of considerations, using various assessment techniques and instruments, including observations by the principal, the teacher, the support staff, and parents."*
>
> —*Early Childhood Education and the Elementary School Principal,* a publication of the National Association of Elementary School Principals.

What to Consider

As indicated in the preceding statement by the National Association of Elementary School Principals, there are now a variety of tests and evaluations—including my own 50-item checklist—that can be used to gather information about a child who is being considered for retention. These "instruments" have differing advantages and disadvantages, and like retention itself, need to be evaluated within the context of the specific situation in which they'll be used. In almost every situation, however, and no matter what evaluation process is used, the following factors and circumstances should be considered.

Chronological Age—As noted earlier in this book, a child who is born close to the cut-off date for school entrance—and is therefore one of the youngest children in a grade—is far more likely to be in the wrong grade and to end up being retained as a result. At the other end of the spectrum, a child who is already one year older than his or her classmates for any reason, including being kept at home for an extra year or having previously been retained, should *not* be retained again. A two-year age difference often creates serious problems for the child, his or her classmates, and their teachers.

Gender–Research data and years of experience confirm that boys tend to develop more slowly than girls. That's why boys are far more likely than girls to be retained and to receive other types of interventions and support services. While some critics have claimed that the preponderance of boys receiving additional learning time shows that retention and other extra-year programs are discriminatory, I believe this evidence shows that school entrance policies based *solely* on chronological age discriminate against boys, and that additional programs and related financial expenditures are then needed to help boys overcome this form of discrimination.

Developmental Readiness–Children of the same age may vary in their rate of development by as much as a year and still be considered normal. However, "normal" is not the same thing as "successful." Children who are developing more slowly may experience continual frustration and failure when attempting to do tasks that they will be able to complete successfully one year later. This sort of lack of developmental readiness is one of the most common causes of wrong grade placement and resulting school failure, even though the intelligence of many late bloomers is average or above. It should also be noted that patterns of late development can sometimes be traced back through previous generations, with now-successful late bloomers begetting little late bloomers of their own.

Physical Size & Ability–Rather than being limited to sports, a child's physical development may directly affect his or her ability to read and write, complete tasks, pay attention, and perform certain mental functions. Children whose physical development is proceeding more slowly than most of their peers' may therefore be *incapable* of succeeding in a particular grade, unless they have more time to develop. In addition, the social and emotional development of such children may also suffer as a result of the way they are treated by their supposed peers on and off the playing field.

Social, Emotional, & Behavioral Problems–This tends to be the area that concerns teachers most, while many parents are more focused on academic issues. The key consideration in regard to retention is the cause of these sorts of problems. If they result from such things as family issues, a chemical imbalance, or a neurological disorder, another year in the same grade is likely to exacerbate the problem. If, however, the social, emotional, or behavioral problems are a *result* of wrong grade placement, retention may be an effective solution.

Prematurity & Low Birth Weight–Numerous studies have shown that these conditions at birth can be linked years later to developmental delays, attentional issues, and poor performance in school. Of course, prematurity and low birth weight are also often linked to poverty and a lack of health insurance, which means that a variety of other factors and circumstances may be contributing to a child's problems at school. Additional time to grow and learn may prove helpful in regard to developmental delays, but other interventions are also likely to be needed in order to deal with other issues.

Exposure to Environmental Hazards–Pre-natal exposure to tobacco smoke, alcohol, illegal drugs, and other toxic substances—as well as post-natal exposure to them—may result in a range of physiological problems that can dramatically affect a child's growth, development, and school performance. In more than a few cases, the exposed students have an extensive array of severe problems which require a corresponding number of interventions and support services, of which retention may be one.

Learning Disabilities–Especially when children are young, a child who has an undiagnosed learning disability often appears to be developmentally young. That's why screening children and using multiple sources of information is so important when making placement decisions. Additional time to learn and grow is *not* the right intervention for a child whose *only* issue is a learning disability. If a child who has a learning disability is *also* developmentally or chronologically young, retention may help when accompanied by appropriate support services for the disability.

Attendance–This is often considered an important factor in regard to retention, and some schools go so far as to automatically consider retention when a child has been absent for more than 15 days. However, absenteeism is frequently a *parental* issue, so the cause of a child's poor attendance must be taken into consideration. When a student misses a large part of the school year for health reasons, such as a serious illness or accident, another year in the same grade may be needed to help the child make up for lost time and recover from the trauma. Other than that, retention may not be effective, because some sort of family-related intervention is more likely to change the underlying cause of the child's absenteeism, and being retained may provide another reason for the child to avoid school.

Linguistic Differences–As noted earlier, children who are learning English as a second language may have trouble learning material needed to succeed in the next grade. However, the real solution in this sort of situation is an effective ESL program. Retention should be recommended if the child is *also* developmentally or chronologically young; or if a child previously fell behind because of a language deficit which has since been corrected, and now can spend an additional year successfully learning the material needed prior to promotion to the next grade level.

Poverty–This can lead to a wide range of educational problems, some of which have already been covered in this section. In other cases, children who grow up in poverty may become candidates for retention simply because they have been "short-changed" of the experiences that lead to academic success, such as exposure to books and access to high-quality preschool and Head Start programs. The best way to overcome this sort of disadvantage is likely to be accelerated learning and extended school days, rather than another year in the same grade, unless the child is *also* developmentally or chronologically young.

Availability of Support Services–As noted elsewhere in this books, budget cutbacks and statistical mandates have reduced the availability of support services in numerous schools, contributing to the growing numbers of "gray-area kids" whose problems cannot be diagnosed or who do not qualify for programs that might help them succeed in school. Retention should *not* be used as a substitute for support services, as it will not solve the underlying problems and is likely to do little more than to prop up struggling students. However, in situations where *no* other alternatives are available, it may be the least educators can do to help students who have fallen so far behind that additional time is needed to master at least some needed skills and information.

Grade Levels & Alternative Programs–Some schools—and even individual classes—have a more intense academic orientation, so a retention decision should always be based on the fit between the child and his or her specific school environment. A child who might have thrived in a play-oriented kindergarten may struggle and fail in an overly academic kindergarten, and this same sort of consideration should be applied to upper grades, as well. Also, as previously mentioned, the existence of alternative extra-year programs may make spending another year in the same grade unnecessary, rather than the *only* way to provide an additional year of growing and learning time.

The Child's Attitude–When a child is adamantly opposed to being retained, he or she will probably be at-risk for a range of problems if forced to spend an extra year in the same grade. However, children who are chronologically or developmentally young—and therefore experiencing problems due to wrong grade placement—*rarely* are adamantly opposed to retention, because to some extent they know they do not belong in their current grade. These sorts of children may have some initial concerns or resistance, which can usually be resolved through discussion with their parents and teacher. Other children may "dig in" and remain opposed to being retained no matter what, at which point an alternative plan may be needed, because the child is likely to do everything possible to "prove" that retention is the wrong approach.

Parental Attitudes–This is probably the most crucial consideration, as it tends to have the most impact on the child. When both parents are strongly opposed to retention—or the only parent in a single-parent family is opposed—retention is destined to fail to create a successful, well-adjusted student. Often, however, a mother senses or strongly believes that an another year in the same grade will help her child, while the father remains opposed. In this sort of situation, I believe the educators involved should present their facts and views, and then encourage the family to discuss and resolve the issue. While many schools do have the right to require a child to spend another year in the same grade, the problems that lead a child to become a candidate for retention are unlikely to be solved without parents' moral support and willingness to help with school work.

Academic Performance–While this might seem to be the most obvious factor in a retention decision, it may actually be the most misleading, because it is more likely to be a *symptom* rather than a cause. If a child's poor academic performance is determined to be the result of wrong grade placement, retention can help. But, if some other factors or circumstances are at the root of academic problems, they need to be identified and remediated. In particular, a problem in one specific academic area—such as reading—should never be the sole basis for a retention decision. Wrong grade placement usually results in a wide variety of problems at school, which is why a reading program or other narrowly focused academic program is rarely an effective substitute for retention.

Putting It All Together

Obviously, obtaining information about all these factors can prove difficult, if not impossible. Parents may consider questions about a child's birth, nutrition, medical care, and other circumstances to be overly intrusive, and they may be deliberately or unconsciously reluctant to provide information about matters such as drug, alcohol, and tobacco use. Educators need to be sensitive to these concerns and explain why the information is so important to the child's education and future success. They then need to be willing to work with the best available information and proceed with what needs to be done.

"Promotion and retention policies are stated in writing, disseminated to all concerned, and followed.

These policies take into account such factors as age, achievement, school adjustment, parental support, alternative programs, and teacher recommendations.

The procedures for retention are clearly specified.

Preventive or remedial programs are provided as soon as their need becomes evident."

—*Standards for Quality Elementary and Middle Schools,* as defined by the National Association of Elementary School Principals.

As this quotation indicates, the process for making and implementing a retention decision should be well-established and understood by all concerned before a final decision is made. The decision-making process, in particular, should be a collaborative effort involving the teacher, appropriate specialists or other members of the support staff, the school's principal, and the child's parents. There should be ample, written documentation of the preceding problems and attempted solutions, as well as the decision-making process itself. The prospect of a child being retained should not be a surprise for anyone, especially the parents, as conferences and other forms of communication during the year should have alerted all concerned to the child's difficulties and the possibility that retention may occur. (More information about communication before and during the decision-making process can be found in Chapter 7.)

Knowing that retention can be an extremely emotional issue—not just a calm decision based solely on the facts—and that the factors and circumstances which lead a child to become a candidate for retention are sometimes so extensive and varied that schools alone cannot solve them all, educators need to do their absolute best for each child but not assume "ownership" of the decision. Retention is often the intervention of last resort and may be the "least worst" choice for a particular student. So, if a parent rejects a strong recommendation—or if a student is retained and continues to struggle and fail—educators must still proceed in a professional manner and do their best for the individual child, along with all the other children in their care.

Parents also have a responsibility to maintain their composure and perspective during the decision-making process, so they make the best possible decision and provide the ongoing support their children need. As always, parents should model the behavior they want their children to imitate; and especially in this situation, parents need to remember that a child who hears them frequently express negativity or hostility toward school personnel is very likely to behave the same way, which can further undermine efforts to solve academic and behavioral problems. Rather than becoming overly concerned about the retention decision and the specific people involved in it, parents need to stay focused on providing the intensified academic and emotional support needed by any child who becomes a candidate for retention.

"We know, because we have data from when these children began school, that the ones who are held back in 1st grade have terrible problems to start with...And so, later on, when children who have been retained do not do well, all of that deficit in performance cannot be attributed to the fact that they've been held back."

—Doris R. Entwisle, sociologist at Johns Hopkins University, discussing her research on Baltimore, MD students, in the December 4, 1996 issue of *Education Week*.

Most—Or Least—Likely To Succeed?

To offer one final bit of assistance for those involved in making difficult retention decisions, following are brief summaries of students for whom retention may not be appropriate, and students more likely to benefit from retention. These profiles should be reviewed with the understanding that—particularly in regard to retention—there are *always* exceptions and there are *no* guarantees.

Learners who *may not* benefit from retention include the following:

Low-ability Students—Students who are doing poorly in school *solely* because of low ability are likely to continue to do poorly even if they spend another year in the same grade. Retention is not an IQ booster, and while additional learning time can help low-ability students master some of the basic information and skills they already needed to learn, as these students proceed through the grades they may soon fall behind again.

Lazy/unmotivated Students—In my long career as an educator, I've only met two students who were *truly* lazy or unmotivated. All the others who *seemed* lazy or unmotivated actually turned out to be depressed or "shut down" for other reasons—usually family matters. Obviously, retention will not solve these sorts of underlying problems, and although some educators think using it as a threat can make students perform or behave better, I do *not* recommend using retention in this way.

Emotionally Disturbed Students–When students are emotionally disturbed or suffer from a behavior disorder, being retained can exacerbate the situation enough to prevent improvements in academic performance. The exception is when a child's emotional or behavior problems *result* from wrong grade placement. One mother of a depressed, nail-biting girl, who was the youngest in her class, told me, "My daughter was normal before she went to school." In this sort of situation, retention can be part of the cure.

Bored Students–Students who are *truly* bored and doing poorly in school may be gifted or talented children whose exceptional abilities have not been recognized or are disguised by other problems. However, many students claim to be bored when in fact they are unable to do the work, in which case retention may or may not be appropriate, depending on the cause of the student's inability.

Transient & High-Absentee Students–Studies suggest that students who frequently miss school or move to new schools are more likely to drop out of school. Retention may make students of this sort even less likely to attend school. And, as noted earlier, transience and high absenteeism are often the result of *parental* problems which retention cannot solve.

"Streetwise" Students–Some elementary school students act like they're 8 going on 17—using language and engaging in behavior most of us didn't experience until we were in high school. Retention won't give these students their childhood innocence back, and it may make them even more determined to show they don't care about school work. Meanwhile, their new, younger classmates will have to deal with a child who is even older and more streetwise than before, and who is unlikely to support other students' pursuit of academic excellence.

Students Suffering From Multiple, Complex Problems–When a student is suffering from a range of problems that extend far beyond the issues additional learning time can address, retention may just create additional problems. Unless being in the wrong grade is one of the primary causes of the child's problems at school, other sorts of interventions that address the child's most pressing problems should be the top priority.

Students Who Have Low Self-esteem–When children have a long-term history of self-esteem problems—or if a child suddenly loses self-esteem because of something unrelated to school—retention can continue the downward momentum and end up being the "icing on the cake." Sometimes, however, a child's self-esteem decreases because of wrong grade placement, and when that happens retention can help.

Students Who Have Unsupportive Parents–When parents actively resist retention—or when parents are so uninvolved they are unlikely to provide needed academic and emotional support—retention can rarely solve a child's academic problems, even if the problems are caused by wrong grade placement. This poses one of the most difficult dilemmas for educators, who should try their best to work with the parents and then let the parents have the ultimate responsibility for their child's future.

Having provided the necessary cautions and qualifications in regard to the types of students listed above, let me emphasize again that there is one type of student who I believe should not be retained under *any* circumstances:

Students Who Are Already One Year Older Than Their Oldest Classmates–*No* students who have already been retained or received an additional year of learning time (even at home) should spend another year in the same grade. When a child is a year older and still experiencing severe school problems, there are undoubtedly other causes that need to be addressed directly. In addition, the social and emotional problems that result from being two years older are very likely to undermine the child's academic performance and have a negative impact on classmates.

Now, let's consider the students *most likely* to benefit from retention:

Chronologically Young Children—When a relative lack of growing and learning time is the primary cause of a student's problems, an additional year in the same grade can be a great help. Children born in the last few months prior to the kindergarten entrance cut-off date (for example, summer-born children when the cut-off date is September 1) would be in this category.

Late Bloomers—Whatever their chronological age relative to their classmates, some children may be developing at a slower but still normal rate. In many cases, the intelligence and abilities of these children are average or above, so an extra year in the same grade can help them reach their true potential, as well as avoid negative attitudes about school and themselves.

Average & High-ability Children—Sometimes, other factors prevent these sorts of children from learning needed information and skills. An extra year in the same grade can then help them catch up, at which point their intelligence and abilities may enable them to experience success in the grades that follow, if the factors that initially caused the school problems have also been dealt with effectively.

Children Who Have Supportive Parents—When a child's parents agree that retention is in the best interests of the child—and the parents are then willing to provide emotional support and help with school work—the child is far more likely to adjust well and achieve academic success. In addition, these sorts of children are also likely to have the good attendance records that support continued success.

Small Children—When children are not doing well in school, fit any of the above categories, and are *also* small for their age, retention is usually less complicated and more likely to succeed. In this sort of situation, parents can see that their child does not fit in physically, as well as in other ways, and that the child would really be happier and more compatible with younger children. Small children themselves are also more likely to share this view.

If a child seems likely to benefit from retention, another important aspect of the decision-making process is the way in which the child would be retained. As explained in the next chapter, retention decisions can and should be implemented in different ways, in order to meet the differing needs of individual students.

Chapter 6

Now What?
The Right Way To Retain Or Socially Promote A Child

If you were retained in the "good old days," it was *your* problem.

Your teacher and parents were likely to blame you for being "lazy," and when the neighborhood wise guys wanted to tease you about not being where you were "supposed" to be, they liked to call you "stupid." Naturally, you ended up feeling like there was something wrong with you for which you were going to be punished until you left school, and that made you all the more eager to leave school as fast as possible.

This negative feeling was reinforced by the way in which retention decisions were communicated and implemented. Often, a child just received a big, red F on his or her final report card at the end of the year, and that meant spending another year in the same room with the same teacher going over the same material in the same way. Usually, there were no consultations, no attempts to accommodate individual needs, no appeals process, and no options. You flunked, and that was that.

Nowadays, we know a lot more about why children end up being retained and what to do about it. Rather than blaming the child, wise educators and parents recognize that wrong grade placement and numerous other factors or circumstances that impede a child's learning are *not* of the child's making. So, especially when the child is young, he or she is much more likely to be a victim than a perpetrator. In addition, many people throughout the community now see a year of additional learning and growing time as a right—rather than a wrong—and as a result, many children are now receiving an additional year during their early childhood. For these and other reasons, taking needed time to learn and grow is a lot less unusual than it used to be.

The way in which children and their parents are informed about retention has also changed for the better, as will be explained further in the next chapter. In this chapter, we'll explore the various ways that a retention decision can be implemented, so that it supports a child's development and academic progress by providing the type of experience most likely to meet the child's individual needs.

Decisions, Decisions...

Having finally decided that retention is the best—or only—choice for an individual child, you're not done yet. You now have an obligation to complete the process by evaluating the next set of options and selecting the most appropriate one. Then, of course, you also have to make the necessary arrangements, monitor their implementation, and periodically re-evaluate how the student is progressing.

But, let's not get ahead of ourselves. First, we need to determine the best way to provide a year of additional learning time before a child proceeds to another grade level. Essentially, that means choosing one of the following five options:

Another Year With The Same Teacher & Curriculum–This traditional approach to retention can work well if the child has a strong, positive relationship with the teacher. This sort of bond usually helps a child learn and perform well in school, and it eliminates the need to spend precious time getting to know one another at the start of the year, because the teacher and student can just pick up where they left off at the end of the previous school year. A child who didn't absorb enough of the curriculum during the previous year is likely to benefit from this approach, which will probably *not* work well if the child (or his or her parents) have a personality conflict with the teacher. It's also important to make sure that the teaching style most frequently used in the classroom is compatible with the child's predominant learning style.

Moving "Sideways" In The Same Grade–In this sort of situation, a student spends another year in the same grade—but with a different teacher. This lets the child get off to a fresh start and experience a different teaching style and presentation of the curriculum. A child likely to benefit from this approach would be someone who experienced an extended personality or style conflict with a teacher, or someone who just needs to move onward but not upward. This approach is likely to work *less* well for a child who is anxious or has difficulty with change or transitions, as somewhat familiar material will constantly be presented and experienced differently, which can be very upsetting for this sort of child.

Repeating A Grade At A Different School–When a child needs an entirely different setting, rather than just a different teacher, another year in the same grade at a new school could be arranged. This could occur at another public school or—finances permitting—a private school. A total change of this sort would be beneficial when a child or the child's parents have had a severe conflict with a number of people at a school, or when a child has become part of the "wrong crowd," or when there's a desire to avoid other students knowing about a retention. Depending on the situation, the child could stay on at the new school or return to the original school after the additional year of learning time. I would *not* recommend this approach for a child who has trouble making friends or doesn't want to be separated from existing, supportive friends.

A Year of Home Schooling–Now that home schooling has become more popular and accepted, a child could have an additional year to grow and learn at home—if there is a supportive parent who can and will meet the child's educational needs. I would recommend this option for a child who would benefit from extensive one-on-one teaching or being part of a very small group. It can also be a good way to meet unusual needs and avoid the pressure and stigma that may develop in a same-school setting. It's *not* a good solution for a "social animal" who craves being with school mates, or for a child who has just a few supportive friends he or she may lose touch with. As with moving to a different school, after the additional year the child can return to the original school or continue with home schooling.

An Additional Year In A Multiage Program–This was discussed as an alternative to retention in Chapter 4, but because this approach usually provides an additional year of learning time in the same room with the same teacher, it probably deserves consideration again here, even though teachers of multiage classes tend to consider children who spend an additional year "keepers" or "remainers"—not "retainers." This approach is good for children who want to stay with the teacher and at least some classmates. It tends to have the least amount of negative impact on a child who needs an additional year, and it is often the most "politically acceptable" way to provide such a year. Obviously, it would *not* be a good idea for a child who seems mismatched with the teacher or numerous classmates.

As noted earlier, some opponents of additional learning time also consider extra-year readiness and transition classes to be a form of retention, even though participating children go to a new classroom in which a new teacher provides a new, higher-level curriculum. Calling this "retention" makes no sense when numerous studies have shown that these classes produce markedly different results than retention— and *no* study I have *ever* seen shows that these classes produce the same results as retention. I therefore refuse to accept the word games being played by ideological extremists intent on pursuing their own political agenda, which has led directly to the destruction of successful local programs and thereby hurt numerous young children. Common sense combined with a basic understanding of the English language and American schools should leave no doubt in anyone's mind about the fundamental difference between these sorts of extra-year classes and actual retention. Here endeth the sermon and this section of the chapter.

Retention Implementation

Now that you've finally made all the necessary decisions about retaining a child, what's the plan for making it happen?

If the type of intervention chosen was considered a form of special education, an Individual Education Plan (IEP) would be required. IEP's are usually written by a child study team that includes the child's teacher, the school psychologist, other specialists, and the child's parents. The plan is based on a detailed evaluation of the child, and it outlines academic and behavioral goals, as well as strategies and techniques that will be used to attain these goals. An IEP is always open to revision and should be reviewed periodically by the team.

This sort of in-depth evaluation and planning has proven to be a very effective way of helping educators, parents, and students work together when intervention is needed, and I therefore recommend using the same approach when a child is retained. An Individual Retention Plan (IRP), created by the same sort of team after an in-depth evaluation, would outline the strategies and techniques designed to help a retained student reach specific academic and behavioral goals. This plan would then be re-evaluated periodically, to determine how the child is progressing and if any changes or additional interventions are needed.

While an IRP requires an additional investment of time and energy in the education of a struggling student, I believe it is both worthwhile and appropriate. Retention is a significant intervention and should not be handled casually or ignored after it has occurred. Forethought, sustained focus, and continued follow-up on the part of educators and parents are essential elements of a successful retention, and an IRP can help make sure that is exactly what happens.

Another important reason for creating an IRP is that retention alone may not be enough for many students, who are likely to need a variety of additional services due to the combination of factors and circumstances which led to their performance problems in school. These sorts of students are likely to need a well-organized and carefully planned "Retention Plus" program, which would meet the other needs that if left untreated might sabotage the beneficial effects of a retention. This same approach would also be appropriate for students who originally were just late bloomers or chronologically young students, but then did not receive the additional learning time they needed at the start of their education, and now are suffering from additional problems as a result. Creating an IRP is an effective way to organize the different aspects of the extensive intervention these sorts of students need, and it can help to establish a system for making sure that the services continue to be provided and re-evaluated as time goes by.

In addition to creating an IRP for each retained student, I strongly recommend that educators routinely conduct statistical studies of students who have been retained, students who participated in alternative programs, and students who were socially promoted. Collecting this sort of data can validate a school's policies and decision-making process, or lead to needed changes. It can also help to refute the statistical manipulation and flawed "meta-analyses" used by ideological extremists trying to prohibit any form of retention for any child under any circumstances in any school.

"After being an administrator in the Erie School District since 1978...I have been quite concerned about the emphasis placed on not retaining students. I believe retention should be [decided] on an individual basis...because of my concern and belief I asked my 1st-5th grade teachers to submit to me a list of [previously retained] students in their classes and how they are presently doing. Over the past 2 years that this survey was done, very few students' grades indicated below average achievement; many students were honor students or well above average."

—Gregory L. Myers, Principal of Burton Elementary School in Erie, PA, in a 1996 letter to the author.

Socially Promoting Students

Based on the information provided in the previous chapter and this one, you may have decided that retention is *not* appropriate for a particular child. A parent or child may be adamantly opposed to retention, or the child may already be one year older than most of his or her classmates, or some other factor or circumstance may make retention an unacceptable choice. And, if none of the alternative programs mentioned in Chapter 4 are available or appropriate, you may then have no choice other than to allow a child to be socially promoted year after year after year.

For some children, social promotion is the "least worst"—or only—option. However, because I believe I have a moral obligation not to lead you astray with pie-in-the-sky "happy talk," I must regretfully state that social promotion poses an extremely difficult problem for educators and the socially promoted students themselves, especially when increased class sizes and budget cuts are effectively *preventing* many educators from providing the individualized instruction and support services that many socially promoted students need and deserve. In particular, after third grade—when the emphasis switches from "learning to read" to "reading to learn"—a child who has not mastered basic skills, or who has fallen far behind for some other reason, may find that many whole-class and even small-group activities are incomprehensible and/or impossible.

Obviously, this sort of child *should* be receiving intensive support services that effectively solve the child's educational problems. Just as a retained child is likely to need "Retention Plus," a socially promoted child is even more likely to need "Social Promotion Plus." In addition to whatever services are appropriate for previously diagnosed problems, educators and parents also have to be prepared for the social and emotional problems that often occur when everyone in the class, including the socially promoted child, knows that he or she is incapable of doing work that most other classmates complete easily. Academic success—and the true self-esteem that grows out of competence and confidence—are unlikely to flourish in this sort of situation.

> *"Some people fear that holding a child back will hurt his feelings and damage his ego...but what could be worse for his self-esteem than not being able to read or solve problems, and being at the bottom of the class?"*

—Louise Bates Ames, Ph.D., in the April, 1994 issue of *Parenting Magazine.*

To deal with the wide range of problems that may lead to or result from social promotion, educators should create an Individual Social Promotion Plan (ISPP) to make sure that needed services are organized, delivered, and re-evaluated over time. Creating an ISPP is particularly important, because an additional year of time to grow and learn may solve a child's educational problems, but social promotion alone almost never does. Requiring an ISPP for each socially promoted child can also be an effective way to discourage the scurrilous practice of forced social promotion, as administrators motivated by financial considerations are unlikely to want to create and sign such a document, when the educators and parents directly responsible for the child oppose it.

When social promotion is done for the right reasons and accompanied by appropriate services, there is a chance the child may achieve a breakthrough and catch up to his or her classmates, more or less. Or, the child may be propped up enough to scrape by. Unfortunately, however, the child may just keep falling further and further behind, even when receiving needed services, because the harsh reality is that educators are not miracle workers, and 180 school days that are each 6 hours long may not be enough to overcome the extensive array of physical, social, emotional and intellectual problems that some children *bring* to school. Educators must do their best, nonetheless, but expecting educators to solve all underlying family and societal problems—or to overcome all physical limitations and developmental patterns—without giving a child needed time to learn is simply unrealistic.

As previously discussed, the factors and circumstances that continue to afflict our student population are likely to prevent many of them from meeting high standards, even if they receive a year of additional learning time. An emphasis on high standards will therefore need to be combined with the development of innovative new programs for students who must continue proceeding through the grades after they have failed to meet high standards. It is, perhaps, fortunate that the politicians, business executives, and other "experts" calling for high standards seem relatively uninterested in this difficult challenge, because I believe the real solutions can only be developed by the concerned educators and parents who work *directly* with children caught in this dilemma day after day after day.

> *"Social promotion, teachers complain, forces them to water down the curriculum and spend more time disciplining students who act up because they can't do the work...Envisioning the impracticalities of ending social promotion is not hard in the huge Los Angeles Unified School District. Among its 650,000 students, fewer than 1% of sixth-, seventh- and eight-graders were held back in the 1994-95*

school year, despite an estimated 30% who had Ds or Fs in one or more academic subjects."

—"Passing Along a Problem?" by Elaine Woo, *The Los Angeles Times*, June 29, 1996.

Whether a child is retained or socially promoted, a vital means of turning the experience into an *opportunity* for success is the communication that occurs among the educators, parents, and children involved. The next—and last—chapter of this book will therefore focus on this topic.

Chapter 7

Teamwork
Keeping The Lines Of Communication Open
& Your Sanity Intact

Now we come to a vitally important topic that I have learned a great deal about—the hard way.

Way back in the 1960s, when I was an elementary school teacher, my district superintendent called me on the phone one day and offered me an opportunity to become "upwardly mobile," by taking over as principal of my school. Knowing that I would be the school's fifth principal in 24 months, I realized that this might also be an opportunity to become "outwardly mobile," but I felt sure that I was different from all the recent casualties and could handle the challenge.

It wasn't long before one of my veteran teachers, who had been teaching at the school longer than I had been alive, came to my office to talk about a problem. She told me about a new family in town and about their tiny, infantile five-year-old child, who was having serious trouble just getting through the day in kindergarten and would in no way, shape, or form be ready to survive—must less thrive—in first grade. Knowing how committed I was to helping children achieve school success, she urged me to meet with the child's parents and explain why their child needed to spend another year in kindergarten.

And, knowing I should do what I was told, I called the parents, had them come to my office, and gave them a detailed explanation of their child's situation, as well as what should be done about it. The child's father then gave me an immediate, detailed answer: "NO!"

Secure in the knowledge that I was the almighty principal and he was just a parent, I immediately began telling him why he had just given me the wrong answer. Before you could say, "Tarzan," we were both yelling, thumping our chests, and jumping up and down in my office. And, when he and his wife stomped out of my office a few minutes later, I ended the meeting on a positive note by shouting after them, "You'll go to the grave with this on your conscience!"

A few days later, I was sitting in my office when the telephone rang. I was still so naive, I answered it. The person on the other end of the line identified himself as my friendly neighborhood school superintendent and then said, "I just had a meeting with two parents who are very unhappy with you. They said you said some terrible things to them."

"Well, they said bad things to me, too," I responded.

The superintendent took a deep breath and said, "I haven't had to deal with a situation like this since I was a playground monitor, and I don't want to have to deal with another one like it."

"Me either," I replied.

"That's good, because now they want to meet with both you and me."

"Great," I said. "I haven't seen them for almost a week."

"You won't have to wait much longer," he said. "They've set up the meeting for 3:30 PM on the Friday before Christmas vacation."

"Well," I said, "that sounds like a nice way to get into the holiday spirit."

So, at 3:29 on Friday I was sitting under my desk and minding my own business, when I began to hear a distant rumble that soon grew to deafening proportions. Gathering up my courage, I peeked out my window and saw an extended caravan pulling into the school parking lot. Due to the small size of my office, we ended up holding the meeting in the cafeteria, because in addition to the district superintendent, the parents had brought with them their lawyer, their pediatrician, an independent psychologist, a stenographer, and a big, muscular, silent guy who appeared to be either a bodyguard or a hit man.

When the meeting ended a few hours later and I dragged myself home with my tail between my legs, my wife had saved some dinner for me, but I had lost my appetite—and my certainty. I had started to wonder whether time to learn really was bad for children, and whether it was already time for my school to find another principal. That night, I dreamed about taking a new job as the principal at an orphanage, where there wouldn't be any parents.

In the days and years that followed, I came to understand that while my evaluation of the child's situation was right, my approach to resolving the situation was wrong. I had tried to force my beliefs on someone who had a different perspective, and when my ideas were rejected, I took it personally rather than professionally, paying a heavy price in the process. I had allowed myself to become emotionally wrought, and in doing so jeopardized the reputation of my school, as well as my own position and the good things I could and would do for many other children.

I have learned that I still have to try my best to help each and every child, so that I can face myself in the mirror every morning and live with myself through the day. But, while I still grieve for failing children—as do so many other caring educators—I know now that I cannot save them all. I have also learned that there are communication strategies and techniques I can use to help me save as many children as I can, and those strategies and techniques are what I want to share with you in the remainder of this chapter.

Educators & Parents Working Together

The way in which educators and parents first begin discussing the possibility of a child's being retained can do much to determine whether the retention is successful—or whether it occurs at all. Beginning the discussion in an empathetic way and keeping it focused on the child's best interests increases the chance of success. Using retention as a threat and taking a hard, self-righteous position increases the likelihood of failure.

Usually, it is the classroom teacher, rather than the parent, who first realizes that a child is becoming a candidate for retention. The teacher then has a responsibility to alert other educators and the parents to this possibility, while still doing everything possible to help the child catch up and succeed. The timing of the first discussion about retention with the parents can pose a bit of a dilemma, because scheduling it early in the year can lead to accusations that the teacher is "giving up" on the child, while waiting until late in the year can result in parents' claiming that they should have been warned much sooner.

For these and other reasons, I believe a teacher's first step should be to alert the school's principal and ask for help in creating an "ad hoc" child study team. This could be composed of the principal or an assistant principal, plus the school psychologist, any relevant specialists, the current teacher, and perhaps a teacher from the next grade level, who can help to evaluate the child's chances for success during the following year. The team's first step should be to evaluate the child and do additional screening for learning disabilities, then make a series of recommendations for helping the child do better at the current grade level.

With this information in hand, a classroom teacher is in a much better position to introduce the possibility of retention to a parent. The teacher will be able to explain the steps that have already been taken, and the plans to help the child during the current school year. The teacher will also be able to cite the opinions of other educators who now have a detailed knowledge of the child's situation, and, if necessary, the teacher can refer parents to them for a "second opinion."

During the initial conversation about retention, the focus should be on the child's current, specific problems at school and what can be done about them. Retention should be presented as a *possible*, additional intervention that may prove necessary in order for the child to learn required material and achieve success in school. The teacher should be prepared for the parent to express surprise and perhaps an emotional, negative reaction. I would try to be sympathetic and understanding, and emphasize that retention may be a *solution* for the child, rather than another problem. In the meantime, the teacher, parent, and child should focus on working together to make day-to-day improvements in the child's performance at school.

Obviously, it's a good idea for the teacher to document relevant conversations with other educators and the parents. And, in the weeks that follow, the teacher should also document what is being done to help the child, and how the child is responding. In particular, the teacher needs to ascertain whether the child is now being put under too much pressure, because excessive stress caused by attempts at remediation can lead to *worsening* performance. This evaluation should be based on further conversation with the parents, as well as the child's classroom performance and the observations of any other school personnel who are working with the child.

By the end of winter, the teacher should have a good idea as to whether the child is likely to need an additional year of learning and growing time. This impression should be confirmed by a review of the relevant documentation at a meeting of the child study team. The team should make a formal recommendation which can then be presented to the parents.

To prepare for a meeting in which a retention recommendation will be made, the teacher should have appropriate documentation from throughout the year, including samples of the child's work, so the parents can see once again the specific types of problems the child has continued to have with school work. It is also very helpful to have supportive information about retention—such as this book—which comes from a source outside the school. This can give parents a better perspective on additional learning time and help keep them from thinking the whole situation is just some sort of conspiracy among "those people" at the local school.

Though extreme, this sort of thinking can actually be part of a fairly standard reaction people go through when faced with any serious loss. I therefore strongly recommend that educators familiarize themselves with the work of Elizabeth Kubler-Ross, who identified the following five stages that may be experienced in this sort of situation: denial, anger, bargaining, depression, and acceptance. In regard to retention, the standard progression of a parent initially opposed to the idea might be to deny that the problem is really so serious, then get angry at the educators for not having solved it, then try to bargain for a compromise solution, then grow depressed about the whole situation, and finally accept the child and the situation as is.

There is not necessarily a set progression or timeframe for this process. Sometimes, a parent stays stuck in the first or second stage. Other parents may move through the stages relatively quickly, but then bounce back if a family member or friend has a very negative reaction. Parents need to give themselves permission and time to work through this process, and educators need to be patient and understanding in order to best help the child.

Of course, some parents will readily accept the recommendation, in which case the educator should be prepared to move on to a discussion of plans to help the child during the summer and in the year ahead. However, another common scenario is that the mother recognizes that retention would be beneficial for the child, but the father refuses to go along with the idea. Educators would be well advised not to be drawn too far into this kind of situation, just as police officers have learned to be especially careful when dealing with domestic disputes. Instead, be prepared to recommend that a neutral third party try to mediate.

Having done all this preparation, try to make the meeting with the parents as relaxed as possible by extending standard courtesies. Do your best to make sure that there will not be interruptions, and arrange the seating so that everyone will be comfortable. Remember that being on opposite sides of a desk or table can create or increase a feeling of distance—or even confrontation. Having some light refreshments available can also help to put people at ease.

Once everyone is comfortably settled, I would recommend that the educator start by explaining the following guidelines for the meeting:

- The purpose of the meeting is to discuss ways to help the child.

- The parents' opinion and knowledge of their child will be an important part of the discussion.

- The educator is going to present a recommendation, but it will be the parents' right and responsibility to make the final decision.

- The educator and other school officials will do their best to respect and support the parents' decision.

- Both the parents and the school officials can change their minds about the situation if new information comes to light at a later date.

- Recommendations presented by anyone at the meeting should be discussed calmly, and a good-faith effort should be made to resolve any disagreements. Otherwise, the meeting can be adjourned and re-scheduled for another time.

A good way to proceed with the conversation is to review the plans that have been implemented during the year (and previous years, if appropriate) to help the child. This can lead into a discussion of the student's current achievements, and where he or she needs to be in order to succeed in the next grade. The educator can then present the child study team's recommendation for helping the child achieve success, along with an explanation of why this is considered the best approach.

When discussing the child and the situation, make sure *not* to use labels or other terms that might be considered inappropriate or inflammatory. The key at this point is to focus on *where* the child is—not *what* the child is—and the amount of time likely to be needed for the child to learn and grow enough to succeed in the next grade. Retention should be discussed in the context of correct grade placement, as well as the need and right of the child to be "re-placed" in a grade where he or she can succeed.

Depending on the situation, it may be appropriate to discuss the way retention has helped other children at the school. And, I have often found it helpful to explain that in my experience children are often *relieved*—not upset—when told they can repeat a grade, because they already know on some level that they don't belong where they are and will now be able to stop trying to do the impossible. I can also honestly say that the vast majority of parents I have spoken with felt in retrospect that giving their child an additional year to grow and learn was the right choice, and many have said, "If we had only known, we would have given our child an extra year much earlier."

After discussing the potential plans and any concerns the parents may have, give the parents a timeframe for making a final decision, but try to avoid giving them a tight deadline. Even if the parents think they know their answer, urge them to take a little time to think things through and to check back if they have any additional questions or concerns. Providing some printed information for the parents to take home can be a good way to wrap up the meeting.

Working With Adults Resistant To Retention

Of course, some parents may have made up their minds long before the start of the meeting, or even before the start of the year. In fact, especially when problem-plagued children reach the upper grades, a few of their parents may be battle-scarred veterans who have more experience with these sort of meetings than the child's current teacher. The problems that result in a child becoming a candidate for retention rarely develop overnight, so the parents are likely to have had months—if not years—to consider various recommendations and warnings.

In more than a few cases, the underlying reason for resistance or refusal has to do with the parents' emotions, rather than the best interests of the child. These emotions may simply be presented as such, or they may be hidden behind seemingly rational objections. In other cases, the parents may have very legitimate, well-thought-out concerns that need and deserve to be discussed and considered. Whatever the situation, educators recommending the retention of a child have a responsibility to be prepared to discuss the following issues:

Stigma & Loss Of Self-Esteem—Many parents are rightfully concerned that a retained child will be singled out and teased about repeating a grade. As noted earlier, this is less likely to occur now than in the past, because of changes in prevailing attitudes and the increasing diversity of the overall student population. Also, educators now have a better understanding of how to prepare the child and other students for the change that will occur.

Nevertheless, it is likely that the child will have to endure some comments or teasing from other children. However, a child who has become a candidate for retention is almost always on the receiving end of similar comments and teasing *already*, because of an ongoing pattern of failure and frustration. If the pattern continues, the child is likely to continue to lose self-esteem and be stigmatized and teased. If, on the other hand, retention is used to correct wrong grade placement and the child then becomes a successful student, he or she will gain true self-esteem and be far better able to resist and refute an occasional comment.

Educators should also be aware that often it is a *parent* who fears being stigmatized and losing self-esteem because of the child's problems. Obviously, how this should be handled depends on the specific situation and people involved. Questions can and probably should be used to elicit the parents' concerns about how a retention would affect them. Then, two key points can be made. The first is that all the concerned adults have a responsibility to do what is best for the child. The second is that retention does *not* stigmatize anyone; people stigmatize other people, and grown-ups who engage in that type of behavior regarding an additional year of education should probably not be allowed to determine a child's future.

Previous Negative Experiences With Retention–Some parents may know other people who have had negative experiences with retention, or a parent may have personally had a bad experience. In particular, because developmental patterns often reoccur in families—and boys are more likely to be retained than girls—a father may have been retained and not want his son to go through the same sort of experience.

In this sort of situation, exploring the previous experience and its specific negative aspects may provide an opportunity to discuss and plan how this situation can be handled differently. Opportunities to talk with other parents or educators who have had more positive experiences with retention can also prove helpful, as can opportunities to talk with parents who declined to approve additional learning time for struggling students. Obviously, you should always obtain permission from other parents before referring someone to them.

"Let's Just Give It One More Year..."–This old refrain is a common delaying tactic, often used by people who don't want to acknowledge the extent of a child's problems, or who hope that the problems will all just go away. In some cases, "promotion on trial"—with the understanding that if sufficient progress does not occur, the child will then be "re-placed" during the coming year or retained at the end of the year—may be an effective and appropriate compromise. Even in this sort of situation, however, the point should be made that usually "sooner is better," because a struggling student will have had less frustration and failure to deal with, and will probably not have as much catching up to do.

"The Research Says..."–As noted earlier, all programs that provide an additional year of learning time for children have been subjected to an extended negative media campaign based primarily on the work of a very small group of university professors, who have frequently cited their own "meta-analyses" of other researchers' data. In regard to alternative extra-year programs like readiness and transition classes, the book, *Real Facts from Real Schools* by James Uphoff, Ed.D., states that these negative meta-analyses included "inaccurate reporting of other people's research, and a reliance on scores of standardized achievement tests administered in the early grades, which the organizations supporting the attacks have at other times denounced as unreliable." In regard to retention, the same researchers' analyses have resulted in claims that defy common sense and widespread experience, like the claim cited on page 3 of this book, in which the researchers assert that, "By ninth grade approximately half of all students in the U.S. have flunked at least one grade (or are no longer in school)."

Unfortunately, the use of flawed and otherwise dubious data has become widespread in education and many other fields in recent years. This had led to repeated cycles of attacks, counter-attacks, and counter-counter-attacks on the part of academicians arguing over obscure statistical and methodological matters which can and do have an important influence on the research results and their interpretation. What should be clear from all this—or must be made clear—is that "*the* research" does *not* say anything, it says many different things, which need to be interpreted and evaluated very carefully in regard to an individual child in a specific school at a particular time.

> *"Of course, contradictory findings about student achievement are nothing new...The question is, how can we tell whether a researcher has reached sound conclusions? The average person can't. The media can't either. Most reporters are not knowledgeable in the field of statistics. In writing about a technical study, they are likely to pick up what researchers claim to have proved and report it as fact—which is like a jury's accepting a lawyer's closing argument as proof. Perhaps the time will come when an impartial organization will evaluate reports of research the way Consumers Union evaluates products."*

—Albert Shanker, President of the United Federation of Teachers, in a September, 1996 paid advertisement entitled "An Important Question."

The difficulties in evaluating and interpreting statistical research are compounded by the tendency of some researchers, reporters, and advocates of a particular point of view to oversimplify and generalize the results of a study. If, for example, researchers found that 80% of the retained students in a study were not reading at grade level two years later, critics of retention might cite it as further "proof" that "retention doesn't work." However, what is really needed to make the study valid is a "control group" of students who have *very* similar problems and backgrounds but did *not* receive an additional year to learn, because 95% of those students might not be reading at grade level two years later, in which case a comparison of both groups would show that retention appears to be a more effective solution, rather than *the* problem.

Moreover, even if 80% of the retained students in a study were not reading at grade level two years later, that would mean 20% of the students were reading at grade level, which is likely to be quite an improvement from where they were two years earlier. So, rather than "proving" that "retention doesn't work," the study might really show that retention actually works very well for one out of every five failing students, which is not such a bad average for children in this sort of situation. And, if your child or student might be one of the 20% for whom retention would be an effective solution, allowing the data on *other* students to determine your decision would be a terrible mistake.

That's why making informed decisions about individual children is so important. Research should not automatically be ignored—especially if it has been compiled by responsible, local educators about children in their school—but it cannot be automatically applied to a particular child, either. Educators and parents must rely primarily on their own firsthand knowledge and experience, rather than "passing the buck" to unknown researchers, who have their own priorities and agendas.

When Parents Take The Lead

So far, the material presented in this part of the chapter has been based on the assumption that retention has been recommended by a team of educators to a parent. However, as noted at various points throughout this book, an educator who believes retention is the best option for an individual child may now face outright opposition—or secretive but very intense pressure—from other educators and administrators. Or, like the parent cited in the Introduction to this book, a parent may believe retention is right for a child but be given the old "let's-give-it-one-more-year" routine, or even experience outright opposition by educators at a school.

In this sort of situation, the first step should be to request a copy of the school's written guidelines on retention, as this can provide the basis for further discussions and action. The parent should be prepared to act as the child's advocate and request the creation of a child study team or similar group to evaluate the child and make specific recommendations. The parent should also be prepared to discuss the issues outlined above and refer people to supportive materials like this book.

If retention is rejected by the educators at a school at which the child will remain, the parent should obtain a written document outlining the alternative steps that will be taken to help the child, and then make sure that the plans are carried out and re-evaluated over time.

Whatever, the situation, the grown-ups involved need to be willing to "agree to disagree" with people resistant to retention. This may be difficult to do when a child's well-being and future are at stake, but we all need to remember that none of us have a monopoly on the truth or can predict the future with 100% accuracy. It's in the child's best interest, as well as our own, to maintain our decency and humility while continuing to strive for what we believe is right.

With that in mind, let's now consider how we can best help children being retained.

Working With Children

The possibility of being retained should not come as a shock to a child, any more than it should to a parent. Instead, this possibility should come as a natural and logical outgrowth of discussions throughout the year about ways to help the child become a more successful and happier student. Ideally, the child's teacher and parents should be having these sorts of discussions with the child, and the discussions should be true *two-way* conversations in which the adults not only listen to the child's explanations and suggestions, but also pay attention to the child's feelings. Focusing solely on academic issues and ignoring their social and emotional aspects is unlikely to lead to an effective solution.

In particular, parents and teachers need to solicit and consider input about the effect of the remediation strategies being used to help the child. If a child is spending afternoons with a tutor, for example, or leaving the class several times a week for a "pull-out" session with a specialist, social and emotional issues may be making the child resistant to working hard at these times. Or, the child may be working as hard as possible but still not achieving needed success, because he or she is not developmentally ready for the work, in which case social and emotional problems are likely to be a result of academic problems, rather than a cause. Obtaining this sort of information is not always easy, but it is a vital part of determining whether retention or alternative strategies will best help the child.

Once the parents have received a retention recommendation, they need to prepare to talk with the child by first working through their own feelings, which may include disappointment, frustration, anger, sadness, or guilt. Talking with another parent, family member, counselor, or some other adult can provide opportunities to express feelings and consider different opinions that should not be part of the conversation with the child. Once this has been done, the parents should arrange a time and place in which they can have a calm, uninterrupted conversation with the child.

Rather than beginning the conversation by explaining what the adults involved think, I would recommend starting with a review of the child's problems during the school year and the efforts that have been made to improve the situation. This should include acknowledgments of the child's intelligence and efforts, and the fact that the child now appears to need more time to learn and grow in order to do the work successfully. When appropriate, a parent can also explain that the child was probably placed in the wrong grade when he or she started school, and this was a mistake made by grown-ups that they would now like the child's help in correcting. Then, a parent can say something like, "That's why we and your teacher would like you to spend another year in (first) grade, and we want to know how you feel about that." Not only does this help the child become an active participant in the conversation, it may provide some unexpected and very valuable information.

Specifically, developmentally young children who have been placed in the wrong grade often express *relief* at the possibility of spending another year in the same grade, because they have tried to do their best but experienced frustration and failure instead of success. Some children may simply *accept* the idea without expressing much feeling about it one way or the other. Another possibility is that the child will feel *torn*, because the child senses this would help academically, but he or she does not want to be separated from friends in the class. Or, there may be an outright *rejection* of the idea, followed by a change of heart or continued resistance.

Obviously, the course of the conversation should then grow out of the child's reaction. A child who is relieved, accepting, or torn should receive reassurance and specific information about what will be done to help the child feel comfortable and achieve academic success during the following year. If a child initially resists the possibility of retention, further exploration and discussion of the child's reasons and feelings are needed. Depending on the situation, if a child is in third grade or above and remains adamantly opposed, I would be inclined to respect the child's feelings. If a child is in second grade or below, I would tend to encourage the parents to do what they and the educators involved think is best, again depending on the severity of the situation.

Children for whom retention is a possibility often want to know what would happen if they remain in the same grade for another year. In particular, they are likely to ask whether they will have to repeat the same material and whether they will "do better" next year. Obviously, the answer to the first question depends on the type of retention being considered. The answer to the second question should reassure the child that he or she will feel less rushed and be better prepared to do well, but will still need to work hard.

Children may also ask whether other children will tease them, and this question provides a good opportunity to discuss this issue. I would recommend telling children that they may be teased sometimes, just as they may be teased if they make a mistake in the classroom or fall on the playground. However, because they are likely to do better in school on a daily basis, they may end up being teased less than they are now, and they will probably feel better about themselves and their school work.

This can and should also lead into a discussion about what will be done to help explain the situation to others. Specifically, it may be helpful for the teacher to lead a discussion in the class—or for an educator or parent to talk to some of the child's friends—about the change that will take place. The emphasis should be on the fact that the child simply needs more time to learn and grow in order to do the work well. This does not mean the child is "dumb," it just means the child has some different needs, like all children do, and is the same as everyone else in many other ways.

A parent will probably need to have the same sort of conversation with members of the child's extended family. And, it may be helpful for the child to talk with or hear about another child who has repeated a grade and is now doing well in school. Most of all, however, parents need to reassure a child that they will "be there" for their child—ready to listen and ready to help—and that they believe the additional learning and growing time will help the child be happier and do better in school. Then, the parents have to follow through with their commitment to help the child.

As part of their support for the child in the days, weeks, and months that follow, parents need to find opportunities to provide approval and praise for what the child does well. When retention is done for the right reasons and in the right way, opportunities to provide approval and praise are likely to become increasingly frequent. Overnight transformations are rare, although they do sometimes occur when a child suddenly switches from the wrong grade into the right grade, but often a noticeable change for the better does occur soon after a retained child recognizes that he or she now *can* do the work that seemed overwhelming or impossible before. This contributes to the child's increasing competence and confidence, creating positive momentum rather than a further downward spiral, so that all those involved are likely to see that an additional year of learning and growing time can mean the difference between school failure and school success.

Conclusion

These days, raising or teaching children is hard enough even when the children are enjoying school and doing well there. When children are continually experiencing frustration and failure in school—and are therefore unhappy—everyone involved has good reason to grieve and question and reflect on what has gone wrong. Then, knowing that childhood is such a precious time, everyone involved needs to get right to work on solving the problems.

I hope this book has convinced you that the true solutions for specific children grow out of adults' firsthand knowledge and extended experience with the child, plus some good old-fashioned common sense. Teachers and parents see every day how different children are from one another, even when the children come from similar circumstances and are about the same age. This understanding and wisdom should give adults confidence to do what is right for individual children. When two children both have shoes which fit badly, for example, a responsible adult does not just automatically give both children new shoes that are one standard size larger. Rather, each child should have his or her feet carefully measured, then be given an appropriate shoe for each foot—and then, if the shoe fits, wear it.

It would be nice to think that this basic and even obvious approach would also be used for something as important as a child's education. Unfortunately, anyone who has reached this point in the book probably understands that school just doesn't work that way for many of America's children. And, instead of trying to help all these children in the exact same way, we need to recognize each child's unique and very special human qualities, and then make a sustained commitment to providing the right kind of help for each individual child.

Appendix

Retention Checklist

Directions: Where indicated, please list the name of the person(s) who provided the information.

1. This student is a: ❏ Boy   ❏ Girl
2. What is your best estimate of this student's ability level?
   ❏ High ability   ❏ Above-average ability   ❏ Average ability   ❏ Low ability
3. Do you and/or the parents/guardians suspect that this student may be a "slower learner" (70-89 IQ range)?   ❏ Yes   ❏ No   ❏ Unsure

Name of the person(s) who provided this information:

_____ Date_____

_____ Date_____

4. Has this student's ability been evaluated with an individually administered IQ test?
   ❏ Yes ❏ No
   If yes, what were the findings?_____

   _____

   _____

5. Does this student have basic academic skills deficiencies?   ❏ Yes   ❏ No

   _____

   _____

   _____

6. Has this student been identified as learning disabled?   ❏ Yes   ❏ No
   If yes, what is the nature of the disability?_____

   _____

   _____

   _____

7. If the answer to question number 6 was No, do you and/or the parent/guardian suspect that this student may have some type of unidentified learning disability?
   ❏ Yes ❏ No   ❏ Unsure
   If yes, please describe:_____

   _____

   _____

8. What is this student's attendance record?
   ❏ Good attendance   ❏ High absenteeism (15 or more days per year)
   Please indicate the student's attendance on the next page:

This student was absent_____ out of _____ school days.

9. If this student has had high absenteeism, was it due to illness or disability? _____

Name of the person(s) who provided this information:

_____ Date_____

_____ Date_____

10. Is this student's family highly transient? (Moved three or more times in five years.)
    ❏ Yes   ❏ No

If yes, how often has the family moved since the student started school?_____

11. Has this student ever skipped a grade?   ❏ Yes   ❏ No

   If yes, please indicate the grade level skipped._____

12. Was this student an early entrant (entered school underage)?   ❏ Yes   ❏ No

13. What was this student's chronological age at the time of school entrance?

   _____Years   _____Months

14. Does this student speak English as a second language?   ❏ Yes   ❏ No

15. Has this student ever had an extra year of learning time in any form? ❏ Yes   ❏ No

   If yes, please indicate if this student:

   ❏ Stayed home an extra year

   ❏ Spent an extra year in a day care or preschool setting

   ❏ Took an extra year in a pre-kindergarten or transition grade

   ❏ Has already been retained in grade

   ❏ Remained an extra year in a multiage classroom

   ❏ Other (please specify)_____

Name of the person(s) who provided this information:

_____ Date_____

_____ Date_____

Student's History Of School Difficulty

16. Has this student experienced significant difficulty in the following programs/grades? Please check all that apply. (N/A=Not applicable)

Preschool	❏ Yes	❏ No	❏ N/A
Day Care	❏ Yes	❏ No	❏ N/A
Head Start	❏ Yes	❏ No	❏ N/A
Pre-kindergarten	❏ Yes	❏ No	❏ N/A
Kindergarten	❏ Yes	❏ No	❏ N/A
Pre-first	❏ Yes	❏ No	❏ N/A
First Grade	❏ Yes	❏ No	❏ N/A
Pre-second	❏ Yes	❏ No	❏ N/A
Second Grade	❏ Yes	❏ No	❏ N/A

Third Grade	❏ Yes	❏ No	❏ N/A
Fourth Grade	❏ Yes	❏ No	❏ N/A
Fifth Grade	❏ Yes	❏ No	❏ N/A
Sixth Grade	❏ Yes	❏ No	❏ N/A
Other_____	❏ Yes	❏ No	❏ N/A

Comments_____

_____

_____

Name of the person(s) who provided this information:

_____ Date_____

_____ Date_____

Health/Well-Being (Optional Questions)

Questions 17-36 cover what may be considered private matters. Parents/guardians are not required to answer any or all of these questions.

17. Do you and/or the parents/guardians think this student exhibits any serious behavior problems such as:

    Frequent defiance of adults?   ❏ Yes   ❏ No

    Aggressive/violent behavior toward others?   ❏ Yes   ❏ No

    Frequent use of inappropriate language?   ❏ Yes   ❏ No

Other? (please specify)_____

_____

_____

Name of the person(s) who provided this information:

_____ Date_____

_____ Date_____

18. Does this student have any serious medical problems, such as:

    Juvenile diabetes?   ❏ Yes   ❏ No

    Asthma?   ❏ Yes   ❏ No

    Allergies?   ❏ Yes   ❏ No

    Other? (please specify)_____

Name of the person(s) who provided this information:

_____ Date_____

_____ Date_____

19. Has this student had any serious childhood illnesses?

    Encephalitis?   ❏ Yes   ❏ No

    Spinal meningitis?   ❏ Yes   ❏ No

    Whooping cough?   ❏ Yes   ❏ No

Other? (please specify)_____

If yes, please describe:_____

_____

_____

Name of the person(s) who provided this information:

_____ Date_____

_____ Date_____

20. Has this students ever suffered a serious childhood accident?   ❑ Yes   ❑ No

If yes, please describe:_____

_____

_____

Name of the person(s) who provided this information:

_____ Date_____

_____ Date_____

21. Is this student's physical development within the normal range for his/her age as deter-
    mined by a physician?   ❑ Yes   ❑ No

Comments_____

_____

_____

Name of the person(s) who provided this information:

_____ Date_____

_____ Date_____

22. Do you and/or the parents/guardians think this student is physically:

    Average size for his/her age?   ❑ Yes   ❑ No   ❑ Unsure

    Small for his/her age?   ❑ Yes   ❑ No   ❑ Unsure

    Large for his/her age?   ❑ Yes   ❑ No   ❑ Unsure

Name of the person(s) who provided this information:

_____ Date_____

_____ Date_____

23. Does this student have any serious physical disability?   ❑ Yes   ❑ No

If yes, please describe:_____

_____

_____

Name of the person(s) who provided this information:

_____ Date_____

_____ Date_____

24. Do you and/or the parents/guardians suspect this student has:

    Vision problems?   ❑ Yes   ❑ No   ❑ Unsure

Auditory problems?　　　　❑ Yes　❑ No　❑ Unsure

If yes, please describe:_____

_____

_____

Name of the person(s) who provided this information:

_____ Date_____

_____ Date_____

25. Does this student's family live at or below the poverty level?　❑ Yes　❑ No

Comments_____

_____

_____

Name of the person(s) who provided this information:

_____ Date_____

_____ Date_____

26. Was this child's birth considered traumatic/difficult?　❑ Yes　❑ No

If yes, please describe:_____

_____

_____

Name of the person(s) who provided this information:

_____ Date_____

_____ Date_____

27. Was this child born with a low birthweight?　❑ Yes　❑ No

　　If yes, please check:

　　　　❑ Low birthweight (5.5 lbs. or less)　❑ Very low birthweight (3.5 lbs. or less)

Comments_____

_____

_____

Name of the person(s) who provided this information:

_____ Date_____

_____ Date_____

28. Was this child born prematurely?　❑ Yes　❑ No

　　If yes, please check:　❑ Premature　❑ Extremely premature (25 weeks or less)

Comments_____

_____

_____

Name of the person(s) who provided this information:

_____ Date_____

_____ Date_____

29. During the pregnancy, was the mother: (check all that apply)

☐ Abusing drugs/alcohol?

☐ Smoking/ exposed to secondhand smoke?

☐ Malnourished?

☐ Exposed to toxic substances (i.e., lead, pesticides, inhalants, etc.)?

☐ Experiencing extreme stress (i.e., traumatized by divorce, abuse, poverty, etc.)?

Comments_____

_____

_____

Name of the person(s) who provided this information:

_____ Date_____

_____ Date_____

30. Has this child ever suffered from malnutrition?   ☐ Yes   ☐ No

Comments_____

_____

_____

Name of the person(s) who provided this information:

_____ Date_____

_____ Date_____

31. Has this child had a traumatic or upsetting experience such as:

Someone close to the child has died.	☐ Yes	☐ No	
The child has witnessed or has been the victim of a violent act.	☐ Yes	☐ No	☐ Unsure
The child's family was or is in crisis. (Going through a divorce, for instance.)	☐ Yes	☐ No	☐ Unsure
Moving to a new home?	☐ Yes	☐ No	
Someone close to the child was or is terminally ill or injured.	☐ Yes	☐ No	

If yes to any of the above, please describe:_____

_____

_____

_____

Name of the person(s) who provided this information:

_____ Date_____

_____ Date_____

32. Do you and/or the parents/guardians suspect the child may be suffering from depression?

☐ Yes   ☐ No   ☐ Unsure at this time

If yes, please describe:_____

_____

_____

Name of the person(s) who provided this information:

_____ Date_____

_____ Date_____

33. If the answer to question number 32 was Yes, what signs of depression does this child display?

Often feels sad	❏ Yes	❏ No
Does not seem to have fun or enjoy school	❏ Yes	❏ No
Does not want to participate in activities	❏ Yes	❏ No
Prefers to be alone	❏ Yes	❏ No
Lacks enthusiasm	❏ Yes	❏ No

If yes, please describe:_____

_____

_____

34. Have you and/or the parents/guardians noticed this student displaying any signs of emotional problems, such as:

Frequent, uncontrolled outbursts?	❏ Yes	❏ No
Withdrawn/unable to relate to others?	❏ Yes	❏ No
Frequent lying to parents/guardians?	❏ Yes	❏ No

Other? (please describe)_____

Name of the person(s) who provided this information:

_____ Date_____

_____ Date_____

35. Do you and/or the parents/guardians feel this student exhibits signs of social problems such as:

Is unable to make or keep friends?	❏ Yes	❏ No
Does not get along with his/her peer group?	❏ Yes	❏ No
Has difficulty sharing/taking turns?	❏ Yes	❏ No
Tends to say or do the wrong thing at the wrong time?	❏ Yes	❏ No

If yes, please describe:_____

_____

_____

Name of the person(s) who provided this information:

_____ Date_____

_____ Date_____

36. What is this student's attitude toward remaining at the same grade level an additional year?

Student supports staying at the same grade level for an additional year.
❑ Yes   ❑ No   ❑ Unsure

Student is opposed to staying at the same grade level an additional year.
❑ Yes   ❑ No   ❑ Unsure

37. Do you and/or the parents/guardians have reason to believe this student has a poor self-concept?   ❑ Yes   ❑ No   ❑ Unsure

If yes, please describe: _____

_____

_____

Name of the person(s) who provided this information:

_____ Date _____

_____ Date _____

38. If the answer was Yes to question number 37, do you and/or the parents/guardians believe this student's poor self-concept is directly related to the student's school difficulty?

❑ Yes   ❑ No   ❑ Unsure

If yes, please describe: _____

_____

_____

Name of the person(s) who provided this information:

_____ Date _____

_____ Date _____

39. Does this student make a solid effort to do his/her school work?
❑ Always   ❑ Most of the time   ❑ Sometimes   ❑ Seldom   ❑ Never

Comments _____

_____

_____

40. How would you describe this student's level of motivation:
❑ Low motivation   ❑ Moderate motivation   ❑ Highly motivated

Comments _____

_____

_____

41. Does this child exhibit signs and signals of school-related stress?   ❑ Yes   ❑ No

If yes, check all stress signs and signals that apply:

At Home - How often does this child:	Often	Rarely	Never
A. Revert to bedwetting:	❑	❑	❑
B. Not want to go to school:	❑	❑	❑

C. Suffer from stomach aches or headaches
particularly in the morning before school: ❑ ❑ ❑

D. Dislike school or complain that
school is "dumb": ❑ ❑ ❑

Name of the person(s) who provided this information:

_____ Date_____

_____ Date_____

In School - How often does this child:	Often	Rarely	Never
E. Want to play with younger children:	❑	❑	❑
F. Miss school:	❑	❑	❑
G. Complain about being bored with schoolwork when in reality he or she cannot do the work:	❑	❑	❑
H. Have difficulty paying attention or staying on task:	❑	❑	❑
I. Have difficulty following the daily routine:	❑	❑	❑
J. Seem unable to shift easily from one task to the next, one adult to the next, one situation to the next:	❑	❑	❑

Name of the person(s) who provided this information:

_____ Date_____

_____ Date_____

In General - How often does this child:	Often	Rarely	Never
K. Become withdrawn:	❑	❑	❑
L. Complain that he/she has no friends:	❑	❑	❑
M. Cry easily and frequently:	❑	❑	❑
N. Seem depressed:	❑	❑	❑
O. Tire quickly:	❑	❑	❑
P. Need constant reassurance and praise:	❑	❑	❑
Q. Feel harried/hurried:	❑	❑	❑
R. Develop a nervous tic (i.e., twitching eye, nervous cough, frequent clearing of the throat, pulling out hair):	❑	❑	❑

If often, please describe:_____

_____

_____

Name of the person(s) who provided this information:

_____ Date_____

_____ Date_____

(Note: All students display some kinds of stress at times. Severe stress is indicated when a child consistently displays several stress signs over an extended period of time.)

Teacher Input

42. In your opinion, is this student assigned to the wrong grade? ❑ Yes ❑ No

Comments_____

_____

_____

43. Do you and/or the parents/guardians think this student is developmentally young for his/her:

Chronological age? ❑ Yes ❑ No ❑ Unsure

Comments_____

_____

_____

Present grade-level placement? ❑ Yes ❑ No ❑ Unsure

Comments_____

_____

_____

Name of the person(s) who provided this information:

_____ Date_____

_____ Date_____

44. Do you and/or the parents/guardians have serious concerns about this student's ability to meet the school's grade-level standards if the student is socially promoted?

❑ Yes ❑ No

Name of the person(s) who provided this information:

_____ Date_____

_____ Date_____

45. Check all intervention strategies and/or programs that have been tried to date:

❑ Accelerated learning   ❑ Remediation

❑ Speech/language support   ❑ Counseling services

❑ Summer school(s)   ❑ Private tutoring

❑ Title I support   ❑ Special education

❑ In-school tutoring   ❑ Other_____

❑ ESL   ❑ Other_____

Please comment on the results of these interventions:

_____

_____

_____

_____

_____

_____

46. What classroom adaptations and modifications have been made to date?

_____

_____

_____

_____

_____

47. Please comment on the results of these classroom adaptations and modifications:

_____

_____

_____

_____

_____

48. Do the following child study team members believe this student is likely to benefit from spending an additional year in grade?

Teacher _____ (name)

   ❑ Yes   ❑ No   ❑ Unsure

Principal _____ (name)

   ❑ Yes   ❑ No   ❑ Unsure

School counselor _____ (name)

   ❑ Yes   ❑ No   ❑ Unsure

School psychologist _____ (name)

   ❑ Yes   ❑ No   ❑ Unsure

Learning specialist _____ (name)

   ❑ Yes   ❑ No   ❑ Unsure

Other _____ (name)

   ❑ Yes   ❑ No   ❑ Unsure

Comments_____

_____

_____

49. Please list additional services that will be provided should this student be retained in grade:

_____

_____

_____

_____

50. What is the parents/guardians' attitude toward having their child remain at the same grade level for an additional year?

❑ They support their child remaining at the same grade level an additional year.

❑ They are unsure at this time about having their child remain at the same grade level an additional year.

❑ They are opposed to having their child remain at the same grade level an additional year.

Comments_____

_____

_____

Name of the person(s) who provided this information:

_____ Date_____

_____ Date_____

Recommendation

51. The child study team recommends that the student:

❑ Be placed in a transitional grade (i.e., pre-first, pre-second, etc.).

❑ Remain another year at the same grade level with the same teacher.

❑ Remain another year at the same grade level with a different teacher.

❑ Remain another year at the same grade level but in a different school setting. (This option may not be possible in some school systems.)

❑ Remain an additional year in a multiage classroom.

❑ Be socially promoted to the next grade level and receive remediation, accelerated learning, or support services.

❑ Be re-placed back one grade level mid-year.

❑ Other (please specify)_____

_____

_____

Notes:

Retention Bill Of Rights

Every child has the right to be assigned to the right grade or program for that child.

Every child has the right, if originally placed in the wrong grade or program, to be retained—or to be re-placed in the right grade or program at any age and at any time.

Every child has the right to be included in a decision about re-placement or retention.

Every child has the right not to be discriminated against, stigmatized, or blamed for needing additional learning time.

Every child has the right to have school records reflect the fact that the child took two years to complete a grade or program, rather than indicate that the child failed.

Every child has the right to be protected from teasing by fellow students.

Every child has the right to be protected from the perils of forced social promotion.

Every child has the right to obtain needed support services, as well as an additional year of learning time.

Every child has the right to be taught by teachers who understand and respect variations in students' developmental readiness and learning rates.

Every child has the right to achieve school success.

Poems By Two Children Who Were Retained

Little Late

I came into the world later than expected,
Walked at one,
Read at four.
At three I learned to open a door.
I started school way too early—
because I'm a little late.
K, 1, and 2 were fairly easy,
I understood.
I learned.
Along came third—I hit a snag.
And fourth was such a drag—
because I'm a little late.
It took two years to do my fifth.
I grew
and I matured.
My first was OK and my second was terrific.
It was not a deadly fate.
Now I'm not a little late.

Jason Smith
Grade 5

I Am Glad

I am glad I made the choice
To retain and remain,
And not put so much stress on my brain,
For I am a December boy.

Joshua Farrington
Grade 8

Bibliography

Albert, Linda. *An Administrator's Guide to Cooperative Discipline*. Circle Pines, MN: American Guidance, 1989.

Albert, Linda. *Cooperative Discipline: How to Manage Your Classroom and Promote Self-Esteem*. Circle Pines, MN: American Guidance, 1996.

Ames, Louise Bates. *What Am I Doing In This Grade?* Rosemont, NJ: Modern Learning Press, 1985.

Ames, Louise Bates. *Your Four-Year-Old: Wild and Wonderful*. New York: Dell, 1980.

Ames, Louise Bates. *Your Five-Year-Old: Sunny and Serene*. New York: Dell, 1979.

Ames, Louise Bates. *Your Six-Year-Old: Defiant but Loving*. New York: Dell, 1979.

Ames, Louise Bates. *Your Seven-Year-Old: Life in a Minor Key*. New York: Dell, 1985.

Ames, Louise Bates. *Your Eight-Year-Old: Lively and Outgoing*. New York: Dell, 1989.

Ames, Louise Bates. *Your Nine-Year-Old: Thoughtful and Mysterious*. New York: Dell, 1990.

Boyer, Ernest. *Ready to Learn: A Mandate for the Nation*. Princeton, NJ: The Foundation for the Advancement of Teaching, 1991.

Brazelton, T. Berry. *Touchpoints: The Essential Reference. Your Child's Emotional and Behavioral Development*. Reading, MA: Addison-Wesley, 1994.

Coletta, Anthony. *Kindergarten Readiness Checklist for Parents*. Rosemont, NJ: Modern Learning Press, 1991.

123

Coletta, Anthony. *What's Best for Kids: A Guide to Developmentally Appropriate Practices for Teachers & Parents of Children Ages 4-8.* Rosemont, NJ: Modern Learning Press, 1991.

Copeland, Edna D., and Love, Valerie L. *Attention Without Tension: A Teacher's Handbook on Attention Disorders (ADHD and ADD).* Atlanta, GA: 3 C's of Childhood, 1990.

Elkind, David. *Parenting Your Teenager.* New York:Ballantine, 1994.

Elkind, David. *The Hurried Child.* Reading, MA: Addison-Wesley, 1981.

Elovson, Allanna. *The Kindergarten Survival Book.* Santa Monica, CA: Parent Ed Resources, 1991.

Forsten, Char. *The Multiyear Lesson Plan Book.* Peterborough, NH: Crystal Springs Books, 1996.

Grant, Jim. *Developmental Education in the 1990s.* Rosemont, NJ: Modern Learning Press, 1991.

Grant, Jim. *Do You Know Where Your Child Is?* Video. Rosemont, NJ: Modern Learning Press, 1985.

Grant, Jim. *"I Hate School!" Some Common-Sense Answers For Educators & Parents Who Want To Know Why & What To Do About It.* Rosemont, NJ: Modern Learning Press, 1994.

Grant, Jim and Azen, Margot. *Every Parent's Owner's Manuals. (Three-, Four-, Five-, Six-, Seven-Year-Old).* Rosemont, NJ: Modern Learning Press.

Grant, Jim and Johnson, Bob. *A Common Sense Guide to Multiage Practices.* Columbus, OH: Teachers' Publishing Group, 1995.

Grant, Jim and Johnson, Bob. *First Grade Readiness Checklist.* Peterborough, NH: Society For Developmental Education, 1997.

Grant, Jim and Johnson, Bob. *Kindergarten Readiness Checklist.* Peterborough, NH: Society For Developmental Education, 1997.

Grant, Jim; Johnson, Bob; and Richardson, Irv. *The Looping Handbook: Teachers and Students Progressing Together.* Peterborough, NH: Crystal Springs Books, 1996.

Grant, Jim; Johnson, Bob; and Richardson, Irv. *Multiage Q & A: 101 Practical Answers to Your Most Pressing Questions.* Peterborough, NH: Crystal Springs Books, 1995.

Grant, Jim; Johnson, Bob; and Richardson, Irv. *Our Best Advice: The Multiage Problem Solving Handbook.* Peterborough, NH: Crystal Springs Books, 1996.

Hallowell, Edward M., and Ratey, John J. *Driven to Distraction.* New York: Touchstone, 1994.

Healy, Jane M. *Endangered Minds: Why Children Don't Think and What We Can Do About It.* New York: Simon and Schuster, 1990.

Healy, Jane M. *Your Child's Growing Mind: A Guide to Learning and Brain Development From Birth to Adolescence.* New York: Doubleday, 1987.

Hobby, Janice Hale. *Staying Back.* Gainesville, FL: Triad, 1990.

Hoffman, Carol. *Reaching & Teaching The Kids Today.* Rosemont, NJ: Modern Learning Press, 1996.

Keshner, Judy. *The Kindergarten Teacher's Very Own Student Observation & Assessment Guide.* Rosemont, NJ: Modern Learning Press, 1996.

Keshner, Judy. *Starting School: A Parent's Guide to the Kindergarten Year.* Rosemont, NJ: Modern Learning Press, 1990.

Lamb, Beth, and Logsdon, Phyllis. *Positively Kindergarten: A Classroom-proven, Theme-based, Developmental Guide for the Kindergarten Teacher.* Rosemont, NJ: Modern Learning Press, 1991.

Moore, Sheila, and Frost, Roon. *The Little Boy Book.* New York: Clarkson N. Potter, 1986.

National Education Commission on Time and Learning. *Prisoners of Time.* Washington, DC: U.S. Government Printing Office, Superintendent of Documents, 1994.

Uphoff, James K. *Real Facts From Real Schools: What You're Not Supposed To Know About School Readiness and Transition Programs.* Rosemont, NJ: Modern Learning Press, 1990, 1995.

Vail, Priscilla. *Emotion: The On-Off Switch for Learning.* Rosemont, NJ: Modern Learning Press, 1994.

Wood, Chip. *Yardsticks: Children in the Classroom Ages 4-14.* Greenfield, MA: Northeast Foundation for Children, 1994.

Index

A
Attention Deficit Disorder 35, 37

C
chronologically young children 9, 25, 29, 34, 38–40, 66–67, 69, 71, 77, 84

D
developmental readiness 34, 43, 67
developmentally appropriate practices 39, 41, 42, 48, 62–63
developmentally young children 25, 29, 34–35, 45, 57, 69, 71, 103

F
first grade 36, 38, 39, 49, 53, 54, 56, 60, 74, 89

K
kindergarten iv, 1, 15, 36–38, 41, 44, 46, 47, 49, 50–53, 56, 57, 59, 70, 77, 89

L
late bloomers 25–27, 32, 45, 47, 49, 51, 52, 58, 61, 67, 77, 84
late learners 26, 47, 51, 52, 57, 58, 59, 61
learning disabilities 25, 27, 35–36, 61, 69, 92
learning disabled 35
learning rate 43, 45
looping 56

M
multiage classes 46, 54–55, 82

N
National Association for the Education of Young Children 9, 40–42, 48, 62
National Education Commission on Time and Learning 5, 28, 33

More Great Books
Available from Modern Learning Press

"I Hate School!"
Some Common-Sense Answers For Educators & Parents
Who Want To Know Why & What To Do About It.
by Jim Grant

Real Facts From Real Schools:
What You're Not Supposed To Know About
School Readiness and Transition Programs.
by James K. Uphoff

The Kindergarten Teacher's Very Own
Student Observation & Assessment Guide.
by Judy Keshner

Starting School: A Parent's Guide to the Kindergarten Year.
by Judy Keshner

Emotion: The On-Off Switch for Learning.
by Priscilla L. Vail

What's Best for Kids:
A Guide to Developmentally Appropriate Practices
for Teachers & Parents of Children Ages 4-8.
by Anthony Coletta

For more information, contact
Modern Learning Press
P.O. Box 167
Rosemont, NJ 08556

or call toll-free
1-800-627-5867